A handful of light

Published by
The Bible Reading Fellowship
15 The Chambers, Vineyard
Abingdon, OX14 3FE
United Kingdom
Tel: +44 (0)1865 319700
Email: enquiries@brf.org.uk
Website: www.brf.org.uk

ISBN 978 1 84101 247 6
First published 2008
10 9 8 7 6 5 4 3 2 1 0
All rights reserved

Acknowledgments
Unless otherwise stated, scripture quotations are taken from The New Revised
Standard Version of the Bible, Anglicized Edition, copyright © 1989, 1995 by
the Division of Christian Education of the National Council of the Churches of
Christ in the USA, and are used by permission. All rights reserved.

Scripture quotations from THE MESSAGE. Copyright © by Eugene H. Peterson
1993, 1994, 1995. Used by permission of NavPress Publishing Group.

Scripture quotations taken from the Holy Bible, New International Version,
copyright © 1973, 1978, 1984 by International Bible Society, are used by
permission of Hodder & Stoughton, a division of Hodder Headline Ltd. All
rights reserved. 'NIV' is a registered trademark of International Bible Society.
UK trademark number 1448790.

Extracts from the Authorized Version of the Bible (The King James Bible), the
rights in which are vested in the Crown, are reproduced by permission of the
Crown's patentee, Cambridge University Press.

A catalogue record for this book is available from the British Library

Printed in Singapore by Craft Print International Ltd

A handful of light

Michael Mitton

Daily Bible readings for Advent and Christmas

For Subhro Prakash Tudu
Bearer of the faith
Dear friend
Hope bringer

Contents

✛

Introduction

On a beautiful and radiant Saturday morning in early June I went to our local shop and was given my usual welcome by Emily and Terry who run it. As I was paying my dues for my daily paper, Terry said, 'This is the kind of day that we think about in those dark days in January, that gives us a reason for carrying on.' I could not have agreed with him more, and returned home walking more slowly, savouring the bright light, warm air, green trees and bright flowers, trying to suck the atmosphere and experience deep into my soul to charge my memory sufficiently so that it will sustain me when those winter months eventually return.

I have to admit to being a person who prefers summer to any other season. I have many friends who love the spring best, and there's no doubt spring comes a close second for me. My wife is one of those who love the autumn, and I do find her enthusiasm for the rich colours of autumn infectious. I don't have many friends who say that their favourite season is the winter. Some of them do speak enthusiastically about winter; I am prepared to believe their enthusiasm is genuine, but I will never quite understand them. Admittedly, there is something very beautiful about a bright, frosty morning, especially when the boughs of the trees have been airbrushed by the cold night air and sparkle in the sharp sunlight. But most days of the winter are not like that. I find I get cross with the grey skies, I don't like the lack of green on the trees, I miss the colours of the flowers, I hate the cold, but most of all I hate the lack of light. In the winter I am someone who needs messages of hope to keep me going.

The Bible readings in this book are written for the season of Advent and Christmas, which, in the northern hemisphere, comes in some of our darkest months. The main message of Advent is hope, and Christmas comes as a festival of light and hope at the time of the year when the nights are longest. Although this book can be read at any time of year, because the Bible stories themselves are not connected with the seasons, most people will probably be following it during the winter month of December and into the New Year until the festival of Epiphany on 6 January. In these winter days, I, for one, will be remembering Terry's wise words and use the memory of that bright June day to sustain me and remind myself that there will be days again when the air is warm and the sun high and, despite all the current evidence to the contrary, better days will come. This is a classic expression of hope: though things are tough now, there is an instinct, a belief, an awareness that there is a better world which we will experience sooner or later. Hope is the fuel that has kept many people going when they have had to face the many and various types of darkness that this world can bring.

Sister Stan is an Irish nun who has written a book of daily readings called *Gardening the Soul*. In her reading for 21 March she writes, 'Hope is daring, courageous; it has the audacity to reach a hand into the darkness and come out with a handful of light.'[1] It reminds me of the following saying that I have come across, which I believe goes right back to the first century AD: 'When you light the lamps in the evening, you say to the darkness, "I beg to differ!"' That custom reveals that wonderful human determination not to let the darkness have the last word. I have come across that determination time and time again throughout my life, and I have never ceased to be moved by it. I often see it in people who are facing what I think must be unbearable strains in their work or homes and press on regardless, some of them even cheerfully; I have seen it in friends who have been bereaved, who have remarkably found energy to haul themselves along the rocky path of grief, not only surviving but discovering treasures on their journey which they have shared with me and others; I have seen it in some internationally known people, those who have carried amazing beacons of light like the courageous Martin Luther King and the compassionate Mother Therea; I have seen it in countless fictional characters in novels and films in which writers and film-makers have used their skills to depict a message of hope that spills out of that story into ours. I have also seen it in the pages of the Bible, and in these coming weeks we shall be looking at some of these ancient stories and discovering the same infectious energy and determination. As I explore the stories of hope in the Bible, in history and in everyday life, I am discovering that hope is a quality that is not just about a better future. It is a quality that has the power to transform the present moment. For me, true hope means that I can somehow find a handful of light even on a January afternoon and allow it to change me from grumpy resignation to joyful acceptance. Now that is good news!

Starting points

The starting point of this book is our common humanity. You do not have to be at a certain level of Christian understanding or maturity to read this book—you just have to be human! I think it is likely that most people reading a book of daily Bible readings will be Christians. But I very much hope that others will also be joining in the journey—those just starting to find faith, those who have lost their faith, and those whose faith seems on the point of extinction.

For the last few years here in Derby, I have been the minister responsible for St Paul's Church, which is situated near the centre of the city. It had not had an easy life in recent times but was kept going by a wonderful and faithful small group of people. In 2003, a few of us from another church joined these folk to help and encourage them, and, little by little, we have seen signs of growth. I have learned so much at this church, not least through our 'Soul Café', an evening event that was held on the first Sunday of the month over three years. It took place in the church but was very different from normal church services. The church was laid out as a café, with a stage where live music, storytelling and poetry took place. There were snippets of films and other multi-media presentations. It included exploration of Christian themes in such a way that they were accessible to all. As a result, we found lots of people coming who would not come to 'normal' church, and one of the exciting results is that they have begun to show us how to 'do church' in a language that non-churchgoers understand. The project is currently continuing as 'Soul Studio'.[2] During these events, I find myself deeply aware of our common humanity—those with faith, those without, and those not sure where they are, all travelling together with a strong sense of mutual respect, and daring to explore together.

I hope something of this exploration will happen in these daily readings, that together we will set out with open hearts and minds to see what we might discover. If you are a regular Bible reader, then many of the passages will be familiar to you, but it's amazing how new treasures can be found in familiar places. Perhaps, however, you are someone who is not a Christian, and you haven't read much of the Bible in your life. Maybe you are reading this because a Christian friend has given it to you as an early Christmas present and you don't want to offend them by not reading it! But you may well be one of those who, somewhere inside, is aware of an instinct telling them that within this book there is a personal message for them. I feel sure that if you read these passages with openness, you won't be disappointed. Whoever you are and wherever you are in your life, we all have one thing in common: we all need hope, and our quest in these weeks ahead is to reach our hand into these ancient scriptures and draw out handfuls of light.

The way the book works is like this: there is a Bible passage for every day, followed by some comments. There are questions to help you reflect on the passage and a prayer that you are welcome to use.

The Bible readings are all related in some way to the two major themes that are celebrated in the Christian Church at this time of year: Advent and Christmas. For those not familiar with these festivals, they mean the following:

Advent: This season looks forward to the coming of Jesus, including his first coming here on earth and also his promised return at the end of this age.

Christmas: This season celebrates the birth of Jesus.

For those reading the book in the Advent and Christmas season, I suggest you start on 1 December, which means that you will complete the readings on the twelfth day of Christmas, the feast of Epiphany, when we remember the fact that God made himself known to us through his Son, Jesus. However, the readings are not especially geared to particular days, so you can be flexible.

Each of these festivals carries a profound and encouraging message of hope, and it is this theme that I will be focusing on in particular. We live in an age when there is much that can tempt us to despair. It may be our ordinary everyday lives, with the pressures of life possibly compounded by financial worries or job insecurity. We may be facing the pain of an ongoing illness in ourselves or in someone we love. We may feel burdened by problems in our local community, and feel close to despair when we see constant acts of vandalism and violence in our neighbourhoods and wonder at what will become of some of our young people. We may feel burdened by the many disturbances in our world brought about by natural disaster or political upheavals. There is much in our often fragile lives that can get us down. But as we shall see, these issues are nothing new; the human family whose stories are described in the pages of the Bible also had their fair share of fear, grief and depression, and in these next few weeks we shall see that the messages of hope that renewed and sustained them also hold good for us today.

Meeting in a group

You may like to use this book for group study (although I appreciate that, if you are studying this at Advent and Christmas, it is not the best time for weekly meetings!) You could meet once a week, after you have completed each week's readings, and share what you have been learning. It would help to make notes of your thoughts, and you might find it helpful to keep a brief journal. The questions for reflection at the end of each day's reading will help you form your response.

At the group meeting, you could structure the meeting around the following questions:

1. Which of the days' readings has meant the most to you? Share what God has been saying to you. Give each person in the group space and opportunity to share their experience.
2. Has there been anything difficult to understand? Others can share their insights to help clarify.
3. Is there something you would like to do in response to what you are learning: personally, in your church, at work, or in your community?

Dedication

I have dedicated this book to Subhro Tudu. I met Subhro when a group of us from St Paul's, Derby, travelled to North India in March 2007 as part of a diocesan partnership visit. We spent two weeks in the Diocese of Eastern Himalaya at the kind invitation of Bishop Naresh Ambala. Our guide for much of this trip was Subhro, who works as the Programme Co-ordinator for the Diocesan Board of Social Services, and he and his colleagues showed us a wonderful range of caring activities in which the church was engaged. We saw agricultural projects, HIV/AIDS care projects, projects to support schools and families, projects in villages to empower local people, tea plantation co-operatives and women's co-operatives. We were taken to many villages where we were welcomed with warmth and generosity, and we sheltered from the sun in simple and beautiful church buildings. Everywhere we went we saw signs of the church making a difference to people who faced serious hardships in their lives. And there, quietly and thoughtfully, was Subhro, full of kindness and wisdom and a deep call from God to bring the good news to the poor in any number of practical ways, always on the lookout for new projects to ease the lives of the people he loves so much. Subhro has become a good friend to us, and he represents that army of people in places of the world that has seen too much despair. They are those who know the stuff that hope is made of. They don't just speak about hope, they do it, and their example is a constant inspiration.

✛

Lament

Much of this book will focus on the opening sections of the Gospels of Matthew, Luke and John. Matthew and Luke give us those well known infancy stories—the angel Gabriel appearing to the young Mary; the birth of Jesus in the musty stable; the curious shepherds and those wise men following their star. These are stories well known to us through Christmas carols, greetings cards and children's nativity plays. We shall also look at the opening lines of the Gospel of John—words we hear if we go to a midnight service. John doesn't give us any of the stories of stables and wise men. Instead, he goes for a much more mystical approach, playing with the concepts of word and light.

Before we get to those stories, we shall have a couple of weeks mostly in the Old Testament, that large body of writing that records stories, teaching and poetry from the days before the coming of Christ. These stories will set the scene for the birth of Jesus and begin to explore the theme of hope. In our first week, however, we are going to think about the theme of *Lament*. Now, I must admit, I thought long and hard about the wisdom of starting a book with lots of readings on the theme of lament. It's not exactly the most cheerful way to begin, and I keep wondering whether readers would prefer a more upbeat start. But no one likes endless stories of a pain-free world with problem-free people living idealized lives. If you have seen the film *Pleasantville*, you'll remember how you felt when the two young people find themselves dramatically transported into a 1950s black-and-white American soap, where everyone lives in a state of relentless cheerfulness. I found it completely sickening! The film beautifully develops the theme of people moving from a superficial, artificial life into reality with its genuine joys as well as painful sorrows, and all the complexities of normal life.

Hope is an important theme to us, precisely because we live in a world where much happens that depresses, puzzles, pains and exhausts us. It is immensely reassuring to discover that the Bible is not a set from *Pleasantville*: a land full of beautiful people leading perfect, smiling lives, solving every problem with breathtaking wisdom, winning every battle and bearing pain with dazzling courage. In this first week of readings we shall discover that there is much suffering recorded in the Bible that does not have quick-fix solutions, and there are many mysteries that are not solved. Time and again I go to my Bible and find myself amongst people who, though living in very different times to ours, nonetheless struggle with similar issues to the ones I face, and ask similar questions to mine.

The word 'lament' feels like quite a powerful word to me. It carries a sense of deep grief, regret, yearning. It's probably not a word we use very often, and I suspect it's used more in religious circles. But the experience of grieving, regret and yearning is experienced by all humans. We'll look at some Bible passages this week that show us how some people have responded to life situations that have caused them to lament, and how, those painful experiences have often been the point at which they have begun to sense the first rays of hope rising in their souls. The theologian Walter Brueggemann asserts that 'only grief permits newness'.[3] If that is the case, then lament is an essential part of hope.

✣

No hiding place

They heard the sound of the Lord God walking in the garden at the time of the evening breeze, and the man and his wife hid themselves from the presence of the Lord God among the trees of the garden. But the Lord God called to the man, and said to him, 'Where are you?' He said, 'I heard the sound of you in the garden, and I was afraid, because I was naked; and I hid myself.' He said, 'Who told you that you were naked? Have you eaten from the tree of which I commanded you not to eat?' The man said, 'The woman whom you gave to be with me, she gave me fruit from the tree, and I ate.' Then the Lord God said to the woman, 'What is this that you have done?' The woman said, 'The serpent tricked me, and I ate.'

GENESIS 3:8–13

The opening two chapters of Genesis are a beautiful description of the creation of the universe. The writer or writers of these verses were not trying to provide a scientific account of the origin of the universe; their intention was to convey through their writing skills some key messages. They were describing their profoundly held belief that the universe was created by God, that he created it in an orderly way and that he created humans to live and work closely with him and to have a distinctive caring role for the planet they were to inhabit. They are also keen to communicate that God created humans with the intention that they should lead perfect lives, living in a perfect world in perfect harmony held together by the perfect love of God. But, just as you are thinking that this state of bliss is unassailable, we discover two problems in these stories. Firstly, there is the existence of evil that threatens the state of perfection. Secondly, humans have been given the freedom to choose either good or evil, and there is within these humans the possibility that they may prefer to choose evil. Without this ability to choose, they would have no personality—they would simply be robots programmed to think and do only good. It is the fact that they have choices that makes them real.

If you read the first two chapters of Genesis, you can't help but feel moved. You have this idyllic scene of God working with the blessed soil of our planet, forming life, developing plants, creating many different forms of life to occupy land, air and water. And he creates a man and a woman. These are not simply other life forms; these, we are told by the writers, are made in 'the image of God' (1:27), and into the nostrils of these creatures God breathes 'the breath of life' (2:7).

These breathed-in images of God settle into their new home, which is a place of great peace and safety until something catastrophic happens. Evil appears in Genesis 3:1, in the form of a serpent, and begins a discussion with the woman, making her aware that she has choice—she can choose good or evil. If that's the case, why not just try a little of the evil, just to see? It can't do you any harm. In fact, try eating from that tree, says the serpent, and you will know everything you ever need to know. As we look at this story, we realize we are reading here not so much a literal story of two people at the beginning of human history; we are reading about ourselves, and that is exactly what the first writers wanted us to see. To start working out if there was a literal Adam and Eve completely misses the point. The point of the story is to declare that God's original design for this world was perfection, but it has been desperately damaged—and not by two people in the Garden of Eden in the long-distant past. It is being desperately damaged by me and you, every time we choose darkness over light, evil over good, selfishness over kindness, deceit over truth.

The writers of this story knew all too well what it felt like to choose dark rather than light. They knew what it was like to do something they knew to be wrong and feel their conscience pricked.

That's why they write the story so well and why it has resonated with millions of people over many centuries. We *know* this story so well in our own experience.

Adam and Eve, the writers, you and me, have chosen to eat forbidden fruit. We thought we knew better. 'Why should God tell us what to do?' we thought. 'We are adults.' In the Genesis story, we read that after they have eaten the forbidden fruit, the man and the woman do feel different. They decide they should cover themselves and they make fig-leaf clothes. Maybe as they are sewing the leaves together they are discussing that the fruit of that tree was really rather tasty, and no harm was done by eating it, and in many ways it was probably very nutritious... until they hear 'the sound of the Lord God walking in the garden at the time of the evening breeze' (v. 8). What a wonderful image this is! It shows us world where God sounds so tenderly human as he wanders around the garden at the end of a hot, sunny day. Amazingly, he appears not to know that the two have eaten the forbidden fruit (v. 11). It seems as if he has deliberately humbled himself so that he can be as near as possible to his human companions.

You get the impression that before the fateful encounter with the serpent, the man and woman and God were often to be found wandering around the garden together, and there's nothing unusual about God turning up to see them in the time of the evening breeze. Only this time, when Adam and Eve hear the sound of his approach, they feel a strange desire to hide. They don't want God to see them; they want to protect themselves—they have already tried to cover up their bodies with fig leaves (v. 7). The beautiful, free, trusting relationship with God has been broken, and they are now in a world where they have something to hide, where they feel ashamed. Then, as they hide in the trees, hoping that God won't see them, they hear that loving, searching voice: 'Where are you?' (v. 9).

Eventually, God finds his companions and Adam says, 'I heard the sound of you in the garden, and I was afraid, because I was naked, and I hid myself' (v. 10). Well, at least he is honest. This sad comment reveals that fear has entered his heart, displacing the love and trust that once happily resided there. Strictly speaking, he is not naked. He is wearing a designer Eden Garden fig-leaf suit! But he still feels naked—and this means more than a lack of clothes. He feels a deep vulnerability. The rest of the story doesn't make for happy reading. Adam blames Eve; Eve blames the serpent; God curses the serpent and explains to the humans the terrible consequences of their actions, which include pain, toil, exhaustion and banishment from the beautiful garden, and the loss of that close companionship with God. In the midst of all this bad news, there is one touching verse (v. 21), in which we are told that God made garments of skin for Adam and Eve and clothed them. Although he is desperately disappointed by their actions, he nonetheless does not lose his love and compassion for them. He looks at the fig-leaf suits and knows they won't adequately protect them, so he makes them garments that are far stronger than fig leaves, so that his friends do not feel quite so naked.

Each time I read this story, I get the sense that there is more sorrow in God's heart than there is in the humans'. When I reach the end of the chapter (v. 24) and see God posting an angel at the entrance of Eden, I see a rather lonely God walking back into his beautiful garden with sad memories of the days when he laughed and played with the man and the woman and they strolled together in the evening breeze, chuckling over the absurd waddle of a duck or delighting in the beautiful colours of a dragonfly wing.

Guilt is a difficult subject. We know the feeling: it's disturbing and unsettling. We know the processes we instinctively go through—trying to make excuses, blaming others, hoping to be better next time, feeling bad about ourselves and so on. If we do get as far as wanting God to forgive us, then we may envisage a rather stern God who is fed up with another human getting it wrong again, who technically forgives us, yet is still cross with us. Maybe a more accurate picture when we experience guilt is that of God's walking back into the garden, grieving over the broken friendship. It is not that we have done wrong that matters most; it is the broken relationship. If we understand that, we will begin to walk a path of hope, because the Gospel stories describe God coming once again to walk with us, not this time in the perfection of Eden, but in the world beyond the garden—the world of hurts, pains, struggles and laments of many kinds. This time it is in our world that he calls out, 'Where are you?' If we take the time to stop and listen, and come out from hiding and dare to say, 'Lord, I am here,' we may well find that a divine hand reaches out and a voice says, 'I'd like to walk with you in the evening breeze. There's much to chat about.'

Reflection

What makes you feel guilty? What goes on in your heart when you feel guilt? Like Adam and Eve, do you try to hide and to shift the blame? Does this story change how you feel about guilt?

Prayer

Lord, let me so delight in walking with you in the evening breeze that I will not want to taste forbidden fruits.

✢

Floods of tears

The Lord saw that the wickedness of humankind was great in the earth, and that every inclination of the thoughts of their hearts was only evil continually. And the Lord was sorry that he had made humankind on the earth, and it grieved him to his heart. So the Lord said, 'I will blot out from the earth the human beings I have created—people together with animals and creeping things and birds of the air, for I am sorry that I have made them.' But Noah found favour in the sight of the Lord.
GENESIS 6:5–8

The story of Genesis progresses, and the humans who once lived in such bliss in the garden of Eden are now strangers in a foreign land. Adam, Eve, Cain and Abel pass into history, and in Genesis 5 we read of others taking the stage—people with wonderful names like Seth, Enosh, Mahalalel, Jared, the very ancient Methuselah and the very well-known Noah. This brings us to a time when there appears to be a very serious social collapse, so much so that we get the terrible verses of today's reading. God, who has lost that close friendship with his friends, nonetheless continues to watch over the growing population of humans with great care and tenderness. However, these humans have strayed now so far from the garden that 'every inclination of the thoughts of their hearts was only evil continually' (v. 5). We then get some verses that I have always found to be among the saddest in the Bible: 'The Lord was sorry that he had made humankind on the earth, and it grieved him to his heart' (v. 6).

The enormity of this is hard to comprehend. The chapters of Genesis up to then have been describing how God decided to make a wonderful universe from formless void. He has created light and separated waters forming mountains and valleys, covering them with every kind of vegetation, and breathing with his Spirit on the earth and sea, creating life forms of many kinds, until finally he reaches the pinnacle of his creation: he creates humans in his own image. There is, in the verses of Genesis 1 and 2, a sense of wonderful delight as God and his images enjoy the glorious creation. But now, only a couple of pages on in our Bibles, we are reading not about a happy, delighted God, but one who bitterly regrets ever creating humans, and who decides to destroy not only the humans but all living creatures. The writer of these verses wants us to be in no doubt—a terrible separation has taken place. A picture is painted of two opposites: on the one side there is the human community, and in their hearts there dwells only evil; on the other side is God, in whose heart dwells only goodness. We know this heart is good and perfect, but it is not the goodness of his heart that is remarked on—it is his grief. It is the kind of grief felt by a parent whose child has turned against them. It is the grief of shattered hope, of harsh disappointment and deep loneliness.

Not for the first time in this unfolding story we are left with feelings of compassion for this Creator God. It is the ongoing theme of yesterday's story, but now things are worse. This is not the lonely God walking back from the garden gate; it is the broken-hearted God who is intending to destroy completely all life from the planet, as he has come to the conclusion that humans are not capable of goodness and now only evil will prevail. He can no longer go on nourishing this community; he must abandon it—blot out all humans and along with them animals, creeping things and birds of the air as well. This sounds like one of those fearful diseases with whole herds of animals having to be slaughtered to eliminate the infection. It's a strange thought that, had God carried out his threat, he would have ended up presiding over a world without any creatures at all. He would have been a lonely botanist, now and again inspecting the odd shrub or tree and sadly remembering his lost companions.

I guess some would feel I am humanizing God too much in all of this, but as I read the Genesis passages, I can't help feeling that the writer is keen that we do acknowledge that God is not a distant, dispassionate deity who lives with his angels in a far-off heaven, issuing instructions, delivering judgments when people behave badly and sending rewards when they have done well. This is a God who wanted to meander with his children in the garden. He is a God who *feels* the pain in his heart when his children have got it wrong. He is a God who has a *heart*. I believe this is one of the key messages these ancient writers were trying to convey to us: we serve a God who is remarkable for the fact that he is in many ways extraordinarily human, while he is clearly not human. We are, after all, made in his image, and so we are related. We share a likeness.

Many people find this rather hard to grasp. Their view of God is that he is more distant than that: because he is God, he is seen to be occupied with major matters and seldom bothers with our normal lives. He may turn up every now and again to bestow blessings, but he can also be conspicuously absent at times when he is desperately needed. Many see him as someone who sends illness and plague and they ask, 'Why has this happened to her, him, me...?' with the implication that they don't deserve such a punishment. So God ends up as a remote, unfriendly, unpredictable, authoritarian figure, who only has relevance at crisis times, and, even then, his involvement is far from reliable. But the God pictured in Genesis is quite different. We have presented to us a God who is intimately interested in the lives he has created, who loves human company, who has constructed the most beautiful world he can imagine for his friends, and who asks in return only that we live by the way of love. Furthermore, we can see a God who is far from dispassionate—he is a being who is capable of grief, of lament.

I for one certainly have my days of wondering about God. The evidence of my particular world at a particular time can cause me to conclude that God at best is rather inefficient, at worst vindictive and unkind. But I find this judgment about God happens at a rather superficial level of my life. It's a bit of me that wants him to know that I'm upset, that I feel I or someone I care about has been badly treated, that things feel very unfair. The steam has to be let off in some way. Then I try to listen at a deeper level, and I realize I am in the presence of a God who also knows what it is to feel desperation, broken-heartedness and regret, and I realize that he understands. When this happens God, for me, is no longer remote, but becomes the friend with whom I can walk not only in the evening breeze or the cool of the day (3:8, NIV), but also in the heat of the moment.

There is a very important 'but' in today's story: 'But Noah found favour in the sight of the Lord' (6:8), and that begins the story of hope in this terrible situation. The story is well known: Noah builds his ark, much to the amusement of his mocking onlookers. Then the rains come and Noah, his family and all the living creatures in the ark are safe and the world, for a time, is rid of the humans who chose darkness over light and is now occupied by good people. God sends the rainbow promising that he will never again threaten such destruction. It is amazing to think that one man managed to persuade God to change his mind, or at least modify his plans so that he would not destroy *all* life on the earth. It is another sign of God wanting to be involved in our world, open to discussion, to listening to us and working with us.

Reflection

How do you find this rather human view of God? What are your instinctive feelings about God when life gets difficult? Do you want to modify your view of him in the light of today's reading?

Prayer

Lord, when floods of various kinds invade the safety of my world, remind me that you are a God who listens and who is never far from planting rainbows in darkened skies.

✧

The last straw

That same day Pharaoh commanded the taskmasters of the people, as well as their supervisors, 'You shall no longer give the people straw to make bricks, as before; let them go and gather straw for themselves. But you shall require of them the same quantity of bricks as they have made previously; do not diminish it, for they are lazy; that is why they cry, "let us go and offer sacrifice to our God." Let heavier work be laid on them; then they will labour at it and pay no attention to deceptive words.'
EXODUS 5:6–9

Today's reading takes us into the story of the Israelites working as slaves in Egypt. The book of Genesis, which started with those creation stories, takes us through many adventures of well-known Bible heroes such as Abraham, Sarah, Isaac and Jacob, as well as Joseph with his 'amazing technicolour dreamcoat'. Genesis ends with the death of Joseph, and when we read of that great leader being embalmed and laid in a coffin in Egypt (Genesis 50:26), we leave the people of God settling happily in a land that honours and respects them. The next book of the Bible, Exodus, tells us that this state of being settled did not last long, however, as the people of Israel were 'fruitful and prolific' (Exodus 1:7), which was good news to the Israelites, but a matter of considerable concern to the Egyptians.

In time Pharaoh became anxious about the fact that the Israelites had become more numerous and powerful than the Egyptians (v. 9) and put them into forced labour. Into this story comes one of the greatest biblical figures—Moses. It is he who is called by God to challenge Pharaoh to 'let my people go' (5:1). Moses' plan is to plead with Pharaoh to let his people go into the wilderness for a short time so they can offer a sacrifice to God. But Pharaoh is not deceived and knows this is really a plan to escape, and he is not keen to lose this very cheap and effective workforce. In fact, he is distinctly annoyed that these people should want to leave Egypt, so he decides to make life even harder for them.

He is currently using the people of Israel to make bricks, used for constructing his great buildings. It is a tough and tedious job to manufacture these bricks out of clay, but it is made a little easier by the fact that they are given supplies of straw, which help bolster the clay and make it go further. Now, however, they will no longer be given straw but will still have to produce the same quantity of bricks. This means they have to make the bricks without straw or go out and find straw—either way the workload has increased dramatically and the mood in the Israelite camp must have been very gloomy. Once they lived comfortably in Egypt, but now they are being brutally treated, and they spend their days enduring hard labour and their nights dreaming of freedom. In time, Moses does manage to lead out his people, but if you had met the people of Israel at this point in the story, you would have encountered a depressed and hurting people who would have felt little reason to hope that their life of bondage would ever come to an end.

This story has been a special one to many people down the ages, especially those caught in the grip of slavery. In 2007 we celebrated the bicentenary of the abolition of slavery, which was passed by Parliament after a long campaign led by William Wilberforce. The slave trade had been a cornerstone of Anglo-American commerce. Many fortunes in old England and New England were derived from the traffic. This trade enjoyed the special protection of the Crown, whose agents persistently vetoed the efforts of colonial legislatores to abolish or restrict it. It is estimated that from 1713 to 1780 over 20,000 slaves were carried annually to America by British and American ships. In 1792 there were 132 ships engaged in the slave trade in Liverpool alone. It is certainly a most terrible and shameful piece of our history. For those thousands of black men and women who were forcibly transported to a foreign land, life must have seemed as terrible as it was for the Israelites in Egypt, but we know from the songs they wrote and sang that they drew inspiration from that ancient story of liberation, comforted that they had companions in former times who understood and had cried out to the same God to set them free.

Thus they sang with real feeling and conviction:

> *When Israel was in Egypt's land,*
> *Let my people go!*
> *Oppressed so hard they could not stand,*
> *Let my people go!*
> *Go down, Moses,*
> *Way down in Egypt's land;*
> *Tell old Pharaoh,*
> *Let my people go!*

The song is a lament expressed with simple words and a tune to match, which must have given great comfort not only to those plantation slaves but also to countless people since who have had their freedom taken from them. But the song is not just a lament. It follows the story of liberation through the battle with Pharaoh, the crossing of the Red Sea and the journey through the desert to the Promised Land. The final verse is triumphant:

> *You'll not get lost in the wilderness*
> *Let my people go.*
> *With a lighted candle in your breast*
> *Let my people go.*

It is a wonderful experience when we encounter those who have lost their freedom and who could be expected to spend their time in endless lament but have not got lost in their personal wilderness and are indeed holding up a lighted candle.

Some years ago when I visited South India as part of a mission team, one of my fellow team members had noticed in the national press the plight of Samantha, a young British woman from the Midlands who had been imprisoned as a result of a drugs offence. She denied the charges but lost her case and found herself incarcerated in an Indian jail for a ten-year sentence. We visited Samantha on a hot afternoon and while we waited for our appointment, we shuddered as we realized how terrible it must be to be imprisoned in a foreign land. How would a young English woman cope with having been in an Indian jail for over a year with the thought of nine more years to come? How had she managed without knowing the language? How was her health on the prison diet and with very poor sanitary conditions? How had she related to the dozen or more companions in her cramped cell, some of whom were guilty of murder?

We thought we would be meeting someone broken in spirit, and yet we found a dignified, humble, thoughtful young woman who had transformed her cell and her fellow prisoners, working on behalf of her fellow inmates to improve the conditions, learning the language so she could relate to them, and working tirelessly to clear her name of the crime she was supposed to have committed. Samantha wasn't a Christian, but she prayed regularly and felt the presence of God very close to her in her cell. Before her incarceration she had worked as a fashion model, but this experience of imprisonment had taught her to invest in the world of the spirit, which enabled her to discover extraordinary resources in her soul to sustain her during this time. When we returned to the UK, we joined in the efforts to secure her release. Within six months she was released.

For me, the thought of physical imprisonment is desperately frightening and I can't imagine flourishing in such a situation. But as I listen to those old spiritual songs and think about Samantha, I realize that God has placed deep in the human spirit an extra-ordinary capacity not only to survive the most difficult of situations but also to flourish.

In 2007 I attended a celebration service marking the anniversary of the abolition of the slave trade. The singing was led by a black gospel choir. Some of the singers came from the Caribbean islands, and their ancestors would have endured slavery. As they sang, I caught sight of that indomitable spirit that had learned to flourish in the most unpromising situations. One of the songs they sang had the simple chorus, 'If God is on our side, it is already better', and they sang this with total conviction. As I joined in the singing and swaying and smiling, I sensed something of the hope that is able to reach out to God in times of great hardship and know that, no matter what, if God is there, things are already getting better.

Reflection

As you look back at the hard times in your life, do you feel as if God was close or far away? If he felt far away, what resources got you through? If he felt close, how did he help you?

Prayer

Thank you, God, that because you are on my side, it is already better.

✛

4 December

Lament for lost life

How the mighty have fallen in the midst of the battle! Jonathan lies slain upon your high places. I am distressed for you, my brother Jonathan; greatly beloved were you to me; your love to me was wonderful, passing the love of women. How the mighty have fallen, and the weapons of war perished!

2 SAMUEL 1:25–27

Today's passage is part of a touching lament by someone who has lost their closest friend. The one who is grieving is David, who became the greatest and most famous king of Israel. The king before him was Saul, who was the first ruler of Israel. For many years Saul ruled well and wisely, but in time he became corrupted by power and jealousy, in particular jealousy of David. Whilst the relationship between David and Saul was strained, David developed a very deep friendship with Saul's son, Jonathan (1 Samuel 20:17). The last chapter of 1 Samuel describes the fatal battle between Israel and the Philistines, and it is during that battle, on Mount Gilboa, that Jonathan was slaughtered, along with his brothers. Saul, knowing himself to be utterly defeated, falls on his sword. The second book of Samuel therefore starts with the tragic situation of the suicide of a once good king, and the death of his sons.

David was not part of that battle but was off dealing with the Amalekites (2 Samuel 1:1). It is on his victorious return that he hears of the carnage on Mount Gilboa and, in response to this devastating news, he writes his painful lament for his former king and his dearest friend. The whole lament is a most beautiful piece of writing and describes the sense of loss that David and the nation feel at the deaths of Saul and Jonathan. The final verses are particularly poignant as David describes his grief for Jonathan. He expresses a depth of love all the more surprising given the context, which is that of remembering those who have died in battle. To have such a human and vulnerable declaration of affection in the midst of a song that declares their fortitude as warriors makes it even more poignant. Yet it is often precisely in the context of shared conflict and suffering that relationships are at their deepest and love is strongest.

I regularly thank God that I have grown up in peace time and that so far my children have enjoyed freedom from direct contact with war. I admire greatly my parents' generation who endured such loss and horror during the Second World War, and, in my father's case, experienced two world wars in his lifetime. But although we currently live in times of relative peace in the UK, wars and rumours of wars are never far away. Since the July 2005 bombings in Londn, we are all too aware of the threat of fanatical terrorists who want to bring war and violence to our streets. At the time of writing, I hear reports of another British serviceman being killed in Iraq. As we look around this fragile globe we hear of so many conflicts; it is such a privilege to be given the opportunity to dwell on this planet that it is hard to comprehend why so many people should want to give their lives to bloodshed and causing suffering. Like it or not, we live in a violent world and at any time there will be those like David, languishing on lonely hillsides, remembering dear friends who have fought by their sides in the heat of battle.

Grief is one of the hardest experiences in life to face and often one of the most difficult in which to find hope. As humans we are made for relationships. We take risks in drawing close to each other, sharing more of ourselves as we get to know one another. In deep friendships, such as the one David and Jonathan knew, there is that sense of safety that enables so much to be shared without judgment or threat of rejection. We invest a great deal in these friendships, so that when they come to an end they cost us hugely. A sudden death is particularly hard to bear because there has been no chance to prepare and no opportunity to say farewell. The experience of such loss can throw us into a vortex of emotions which can erupt at any moment. As we work through these emotions, we have to learn to live without the friendship that was so foundational for our lives.

When C.S. Lewis lost his wife, Joy, he wrote about his experience in a book that he called *A Grief Observed*. First published anonymously, this book has over the years been a great gift to many who have journeyed through the valley of grief, not least because here was a man, a prominent Christian, daring to own his personal struggles of faith and hope in the face of cruel grief. What he found particularly difficult to bear were the people who felt he should be 'getting over it'. He writes,

To say the patient is getting over it after an operation for appendicitis is one thing: after he's had his leg off is quite another. After that operation either the wounded stump heals or the man dies. If it heals, the fierce continuous pain will stop. Presently he'll get back his strength and be able to stump about on his wooden leg. He has 'got over it'. But he will probably have recurrent pains in the stump all his life, and perhaps pretty bad ones; and he will always be a one-legged man. There will be hardly a moment when he forgets it... At present I am learning to get about on crutches. Perhaps I shall presently be given a wooden leg. But I shall never be a biped again.'[4]

Paradoxically, accepting that life will not be the same again is the beginning of hope. It brings to an end the struggle to try to recapture what we once had and starts an exploration into what life might be like without the former love. I have been close to many who have suffered such losses in their lives, and I find myself full of admiration as I look at how they, little by little, find ways of living their lives in different ways. Some years ago some good friends of mine lost their son in tragic circumstances. I felt completely lost for words as I pondered their terrible pain, and spent ages choosing a card to send and anxiously gripped my unmoving pen, unable to think what to write. I then sensed the presence of God and some words came to me. Such words always feel inadequate, but they make a start and I managed to connect with that deep instinct that told me no matter how dark the valley, there is a God who hears our cries:

> *There is a God whose light shines in every darkness*
> *There is a God who hears every lament*
> *There is a God who transforms even the deepest grief*
> *Therefore you have hope:*
> *You shall sing again, but with a different tune*
> *You shall dance again, but with a different step*
> *You shall laugh again, but with a different breath*
> *Not yet, but one day,*
> *For there is a God who heals your wound with the gentlest hand.*[5]

Reflection

Think back on a bereavement you have experienced. What helped you travel through that time? How did you change? How did you experience God through that time? Did he seem close or absent?

Prayer

Lord of the living and the dead, I thank you for all those I love and who have loved me. Some have now left this life, and I carry in my soul the wounds of that parting, but I remember today with thanksgiving that it was better to have loved and lost than never to have loved at all.

5 December

Facing calamity

How lonely sits the city that once was full of people! How like a widow she
has become, she that was great among the nations! She that was a princess
among the provinces has become a vassal. She weeps bitterly in the night,
with tears on her cheeks; among all her lovers she has no one to comfort
her; all her friends have dealt treacherously with her, they have become her
enemies.
LAMENTATIONS 1:1–2

The book of Lamentations has to be the most miserable book in the
Bible! That's not to say it's without hope, but the bulk of it is an
unmitigated expression of misery. If you are feeling cheerful and in a
good mood, then I don't advise reading it. If however, life is proving
difficult for you, then it might be worth a read because at least it tells
you that you are not alone. Victor Meldrew from the TV series *One
Foot in the Grave* was the nation's favourite grumpy old man, and the
reason so many of us loved him was because here was someone who,
like us, also had days when everything seemed to be against him, the
world was full of the most irritating people, and every attempt made
to improve things turned sour. For Victor such days, alas, happened
to be every day of his life; thankfully for us, it is only some days.

For the people of Israel, the book of Lamentations became a book
for such days. We don't know for certain who wrote it, but it is closely
linked with the book of Jeremiah and relates to the catastrophe of the
fall of Jerusalem in 586BC described by that prophet in his book.
Lamentations is an attempt to put into words the depth of loss and
sorrow at the fall of that great city and the exile of its inhabitants to a
strange and hostile land. It is an exquisitely crafted book made up of

five laments, each one containing 22 verses (except the third, which has 66 verses), reflecting the number of letters in the Hebrew alphabet. Orthodox Jews have read this book aloud on the anniversary of the traditional date of the destruction of Solomon's temple. It is also often recited at the 'Wailing Wall' (a remnant of the wall of the Second Temple, now a place of prayer for Jews) in Jerusalem. In some churches it is read during the last three days of Holy Week.

The content of this book is fairly horrific: it describes wholesale devastation and slaughter of kings, princes, priests and commoners, starvation and acts of desperate cannibalism and the forced imprisonment and exile of thousands of people. For the writer of Lamentations, all this suffering is not some random act in the lives of his people but a direct result of their sin (see, for example, v. 5). As a result, the book ends with an acknowledgment of responsibility, and the concluding words are a plea to God to forgive and restore his people:

But you, O Lord, reign for ever; your throne endures to all generations. Why have you forgotten us completely? Why have you forsaken us these many days? Restore us to yourself, O Lord, that we may be restored; renew our days as of old—unless you have utterly rejected us, and are angry with us beyond measure.
LAMENTATIONS 5:19–22

These verses carry a real anxiety that God may be angry with his people beyond measure; if that were to be the case, then there would be no hope of recovery. However, Lamentations is not completely without hope. There is a crucial passage right in the middle of the book, which reads:

But this I call to mind, and therefore I have hope: The steadfast love of the Lord never ceases, his mercies never come to an end; they are new every morning; great is your faithfulness.
LAMENTATIONS 3.21–23

If you are reading the book through, these verses take you quite by surprise. You feel as if you are drowning in a beautiful yet painful poem of lament, and then these verses suddenly push you up to the surface and you can breathe again. The poet is deliberately painting as grim a picture as he can, so you can be in no doubt that this is the worst possible predicament in which humans can be. And then comes one of the great biblical 'but's: 'But this I call to mind...', and that calling to mind is a very important discipline. It is a calling out, a mental SOS for one of the most effective and reliable lifelines. It is the lifeline of the truth that the love of God is utterly steadfast and that he is completely merciful, willing to forgive even the worst offence; his is not an old, tired love—it is new every morning. The writer of Lamentations, who almost certainly lived through the time of horror described, has placed these verses right at the heart of his lamentation. They are intended to colour all that comes before and goes after them. It's as if the poet is saying, 'We still feel keenly our pain, our remorse, our loneliness and our lostness, but we are not without hope.'

It's so good that these verses come in the middle rather than at the end of Lamentations. If they came at the end, it would seem like a kind of fairy-tale, happy-ever-after story. Yes, they were sad, but they had faith and it was all right in the end. No, they are not all right in the end; they are still hurting and longing. But right there in the hurt and the anxiety and the longing there is hope. It's mixed in, not tacked on at the end.

We may never personally know anything like the catalogue of horrors described in this disturbing book, yet we all have times in our lives when everything seems to be much more struggle than ease. Even if my life is going reasonably well, I am almost certainly close to someone who is facing a personal crisis or serious stress of one kind or another. For anyone travelling through such times, there is comfort in knowing that hope can be found in the middle of lament. It will need us to do some 'calling to mind', a discipline that requires us to step out for a moment from the emotional whirlpool where the stresses of life have thrown us and grasp hold of a simple truth: the steadfast love of the Lord does not give up. There is enough of it to be fresh for you today. Whether you are a giant in faith, frail of faith or a sceptic, there is nothing to stop you pausing and doing some calling to mind. When your mind has grasped this truth, let it sink down into your heart and do its work of hope.

Reflection

Meditate on those verses from Lamentations 3:21–23, and in particular dwell on the words that are in bold:

But this I call to mind, and therefore I have **hope**: The **steadfast love** of the Lord **never ceases**, his **mercies** never come to an end; they are **new every** morning; **great** is your **faithfulness**.

Prayer

In my laments, O Lord, I call to mind the knowledge that your love is steadfast. Visit my soul this new day that I may know just how great your faithfulness is.

✣

The Real Absence of God

My God, my God, why have you forsaken me? Why are you so far from helping me, from the words of my groaning? O my God, I cry by day, but you do not answer; and by night, but find no rest.
PSALM 22:1-2

The season of Advent is traditionally a time when we think about the coming of God to earth. This is what the word 'advent' literally means. It comes from the Latin *advenio*, meaning 'to come to, to arrive', and can also be used to mean 'to come near, to happen, to break out'. It's all about God breaking out of heaven at a particular time and coming to earth in the person of Jesus, and soon we shall be getting into those stories. Before we do that, we shall be looking at that uncomfortable experience in life when God does not seem to be on his way at all. In fact, if anything, it feels as if he has hurried back to heaven and locked the door with no intention of returning.

There is so much that is comforting about the Psalms. You read them and realize they were written by people who felt wonderfully free not only to offer lavish praise to the God they loved so much, but also to ask the most penetrating questions of him and even to shake their fists at him in anguish and anger. Today's psalm is one that is very well known, as it is quoted by Jesus on the cross (Matthew 27:46). But we are not going to think about Jesus on the cross today, because, significant though it is that he used this psalm, these verses also have meaning for ordinary mortals going about their earthly lives.

In the introductory note in the original Hebrew text we are told that this is a psalm written by David. The title of this psalm is 'Plea for Deliverance from Suffering and Hostility'. It is written 'To the leader' and is to be sung to the tune of 'The Deer of the Dawn'. There is something very endearing about David. On the one hand he was the stuff real heroes are made of: a fantastic warrior, a great leader, a handsome man and a wise ruler. On the other hand he was also very flawed, seen not least in his fatal attraction to the beautiful Bathsheba (fatal, that is, not for David, but for Uriah, the unfortunate husband of Bathsheba for whom David arranged an untimely death—see 2 Samuel 11 for the full story). The writers of the life of David don't try to hide his mistakes from us, and similarly the compilers of the psalms don't hide those psalms that speak of human mistakes and anguish. We don't know for certain who wrote this Psalm, but if it wasn't by David, it was by someone who was quite happy to attribute it to him and who was happy for us to know that David, although he was a great man of faith, had his times when God seemed uncomfortably distant.

The presence and absence of God is something that has always puzzled people. Trying to describe what it means to 'feel God close' takes a bit of doing, and there is nothing to verify experience in this way. Essentially it happens in the world of feelings and is a kind of intuition. Whatever it is, most people of faith will testify to the fact that there are times when God feels close and other times when he seems distant. Most of us can accept this, but it gets difficult when he appears distant at those times when we most need him to be close. I suspect the context of this psalm was just one such occasion. Here is David (or another person of faith, if it's not him) needing God to be close at an important time in his life, and instead it feels as if God has completely forsaken him and is so far away that he can no longer save him and is unable to hear the groans uttered by this desperate man. He cries out day and night, but all he gets from heaven is a cold silence. Although he could really do with help, it seems that God is busy doing other things.

Some churches talk about the 'Real Presence' of God in the sacrament of Communion. But even in devout services of Holy

Communion where he is meant to be so close, God can seem a million miles away. The writer Frederick Buechner describes this dilemma:

The world hides God from us, or we hide ourselves from God, or for reasons of his own, God hides himself from us, but however you account for it, he is often more conspicuous by his absence than by his presence, and his absence is much of what we labour under and are heavy laden by. Just as sacramental theology speaks of a doctrine of the Real Presence, maybe it should speak also of a doctrine of the Real Absence because absence can be sacramental too, a door left open, a chamber of the heart kept ready and waiting.[6]

For me there is real hope in these words: 'Absence can be sacramental too.' I like the feel of that, but what does it actually mean? I was taught that a sacrament is an 'outward visible sign of an inward and spiritual grace' (not the easiest of concepts to understand at the best of times). If that is the case, then what kind of 'inward and spiritual grace' is signified by the sense of God's absence? If God feels absent to me, my first conclusion is that at best he is not interested and at worst he doesn't exist. Maybe, as ever, I need to look a bit closer at this apparent conundrum. I could go down the path of 'well, you can't rely on your feelings, you must simply believe the facts', which is all very well, but the fact is that I do actually need to feel that God is close at important times, just as I need my friends and family close. So what is this 'inward and spiritual grace' of absence? You are probably reading this thinking, 'Any minute now he will tell us the answer, like that scene at the end of the *Poirot* films, where David Suchet as Poirot spreads out the facts and the sequence of events and then solves the mystery.' Would that I were the spiritual equivalent of Hercule Poirot! But no, I don't know the answer. I am simply someone like you, and someone like David, and we all have our times of crying out in pain and frustration, 'My God, why have you forsaken me...?'

Do you see what is happening as we explore this theme? If there were 'seven easy steps to discovering the presence of God in times of desolation', I would give them to you and you might be very impressed and would try them out, probably on your own. But David made no attempt to take this approach, because he knew this was not the way of solving the problem. What is happening to us today as we wrestle with the presence/absence of God issue is that we are getting closer to one another. Rather than my telling you, it has now become a matter of 'us'. This is a question not for individuals but for the faith community, and it is one that actually builds community. If you start talking with someone else about your struggle with the apparent absence of God, and they say, 'I have that experience, too,' you will probably feel like hugging them! In a few moments you will be likely to feel really quite close to them—here is a friend who shares the same struggle. In time you find there are actually quite a few of you, including the odd person who writes books like this one you are reading, and kings in ancient times who wrote psalms. All sorts of people have this problem. As we share openly together we sense there is someone listening to our conversation. Here is my paraphrase of John 20:19 to try to help explain this:

On that day, when it was dark and the disciples were huddled together feeling lost and afraid and desperately missing their Lord, they suddenly discovered Jesus was with them and, standing right in the middle of them, he said to them, 'My peace is with you', and it was.

There will be times when we long for the advent, the coming of Jesus, especially when life is difficult, and there will be times when we encounter not the presence, but the unwelcome absence of God. Those are the times to do what David did, which was not to hide away on his own, but to talk about it to the apparently distant God, and also talk to others, to share experience, to feel human warmth and contact. It is most likely that before long the risen Jesus will make his presence felt. To force it or hurry it will mean that you will miss his personal word of peace for your soul.

Reflection

As your reflect on your life, can you see patterns or seasons when God feels close and when he feels absent? What has helped you regain a sense of his presence? If he feels absent at the moment, is there someone with whome you can share this experience?

Prayer

Lord, for the times when you are close, thank you. For the times when you are absent, lead me to those places where you can surprise me with your presence and bring me your word of peace.

⚜

To laugh at gilded butterflies

About midnight Paul and Silas were praying and singing hymns to God, and the prisoners were listening to them. Suddenly there was an earthquake, so violent that the foundations of the prison were shaken; and immediately all the doors were opened and everyone's chains were unfastened.

ACTS 16:25–26

I'm ending this 'lament' section with a passage about prison. Thankfully, I have never been held in a literal prison and only ever once visited one and that was enough to convince me to abide by the law as best I know how. The thought of having my freedom taken away is abhorrent to me, and I am always disturbed by stories of those who have been unjustly imprisoned either as hostages or through miscarriages of justice. From these, however, emerge some immensely courageous stories and you have only to think of people like Dietrich Bonhoeffer or Brian Keenan or Aun Sun Suu Kyii to know that the human spirit is capable of extraordinary creative life despite being robbed of its freedom.

Today's passage takes us to the New Testament story of Paul and Silas who are on their travels taking the gospel around the Mediterranean. On this occasion we find them in Philippi. While there, they encounter a slave girl who has occult powers. She is owned by some unscrupulous people who have made much money from her fortune telling. However, she receives the gospel and is freed from the occult forces, much to the anger of her owners, who drag Paul and Silas before the magistrates claiming that they are disturbing the peace. Despite the thoroughly unfair accusations, the two evangelists are flogged and thrown into jail. We read those words quite casually, but such beatings were terrible, and it was not uncommon for people to die from the wounds caused by flogging. So these two men would have been in real pain as they slumped in their prison cell, their only crime freeing a poor slave girl from her oppression.

I know that, if this had happened to me, I would have been huddled in that cell, feeling very afraid as I nursed my wounds and longed for freedom. This is not how we find Paul and Silas! Luke, the writer of the Acts of the Apostles, tells us that at midnight these two wounded soldiers were praying and singing hymns. It must have sounded extraordinary: the sounds usually echoing round the jail would have been the oaths and cursing of drunken men, and the groans of those who had been beaten. Paul and Silas were made of very different stuff. God had got so deep into their lives, that neither the brutal beatings nor prison bars could prevent them from singing their love songs to their Father in heaven and looking to him for help. And help he did in a most dramatic way, for the rest of the chapter describes an earthquake that shook the prison to its foundations and enabled all the prisoners to go free. Not only that, but the prison guard was gloriously converted and in a touching scene (vv. 33–34), we find Paul and Silas in the jailor's house, where, far from imprisoning them again, he is now washing their wounds and feeding them a fine meal; they in return wash him and his family in the waters of baptism. There are many freedoms in this story.

In my reading over the past year, I have twice come across books referring to Shakespeare's King Lear, which has reawakened my love for that grim yet wonderful play. It is a tragedy and most of the characters die at the end, but as the story unfolds the real heroes of the play make some vital discoveries about life. They learn fully and truly to live before they die, which is better than living a long life badly. King Lear himself has much to learn in this respect and towards the end we have a scene in which he and his beloved daughter Cordelia are about to be taken off to prison. It is a desperate situation: Cordelia is frightened and guards are shouting and hustling the old king when he puts up his hand and stops the commotion for a moment. He looks at his daughter who, he now realizes, has always loved him faithfully, and he delivers a most wonderful and touching speech:

> *Come, let's away to prison:*
> *We two alone will sing like birds i' the cage;*
> *When thou dost ask me blessing I'll kneel down*
> *And ask of thee forgiveness; so we'll live,*
> *And pray, and sing, and tell old tales, and laugh*
> *At gilded butterflies, and hear poor rogues*
> *Talk of court news; and we'll talk with them too*
> *Who loses and who wins; who's in, who's out*
> *And take upon's the mystery of things*
> *As if we were God's spies: and we'll wear out*
> *In a wall'd prison packs and sects of great ones*
> *That ebb and flow by the moon.*[7]

In his book *The Enduring Melody*, Michael Mayne, writing at a time when he was battling with terminal cancer, uses this passage as an inspiring resource for facing old age.[8] I hope when I enter that stage of life I remember to read it again, as I can see it would inspire me, too. But I can also see that it is inspiring for any moment in life when it feels as if, for whatever reason, we are facing some kind of imprisonment. So much can happen that can give us the experience of being robbed of freedom: ongoing sickness, a difficult boss at work, an unfulfilling occupation, problems in church, debt, relationship breakdowns, to name but a few. So many circumstances can make us feel hemmed in, and it can seem that forces beyond our control are taking us away to a metaphorical prison. Old King Lear's words can help to guide us here. He has suffered much through the days described in the play, and now his life is to end in jail. But far from letting it send him into a lengthy lament, Lear suddenly has a twinkle in his eye, and, stepping forward to the edge of the stage, amazes us all with a speech of extraordinary wisdom and hope. He looks into the anxious eyes of his daughter and says, 'Come on, let's go to this prison to be truly free.' They may be in a cage, but they will sing; they may have had their problems in the past, but this prison will be the place where they will love each other and find forgiveness. There, they will sit together and listen to the court gossip and realize that those who are caught up in the stress and absurdity of political and celebrity life are those who are really imprisoned. And there they will start seeing as they have never seen before—'as if we were God's spies'. If ever there was a song of hope it is here.

In the end, the old king and his daughter die and so experience a different freedom. But none of that undermines the expression of hope in his speech. It is encouraging to think that the very circumstances that bind us might actually be providing the context for us to sing new songs and see life from a much wiser perspective.

Reflection

What circumstances are you facing that feel as if they are imprisoning you in some way? Have a look at King Lear's speech again. Which parts of it move you and why?

Prayer

Lord, you gave to Paul and Silas songs to sing in the night in their prison cells. When the circumstances of my life hem me in and my soul feels imprisoned, help me to find songs that I can sing. Lift my soul that I may laugh at the gilded butterflies you send my way and have eyes to look beyond prison bars to glimpse the scenery of heaven.

Week 2

Longing

Lament and longing are close relatives. Lament can happen when something we have longed for fails to happen and longing can be birthed in the dark night of lament.

A young supporter watches his team's straining every muscle and using all their skill to win the vital match. Winning means promotion to the Premiership and a world of which he has always dreamed. His team is the one that too often bounced along the bottom of the league, but now it has a chance of winning, and he zips and unzips his jacket nervously as the striker has the ball at his feet. He feels the longing in his heart physically as the blood pumps hard through his veins. All his longings are focused on that player, on that boot, on that goal which is now just one magical kick away. But then it ends. The ball is snatched away from that boot, on to another. The enemy strikes back and, to his horror, the young supporter watches the ball heading in the other direction, and cold dread now replaces excited anticipation. How terrible the cries of triumph from the other side of the ground as the ball enters the wrong net! He had hoped with every atom of hope his young frame possessed. The whistle blows, the end has come and his breath is used not for cries of delight but for sighs of confusion and sorrow. Within a few moments he has travelled from longing to lament, but it will only be a matter of time before the longings stir in his heart again.

It happens the other way, too. She had invested so much in the relationship. She had given everything and had risked all. He had brought out the best in her, and there were days when it felt as if she was walking in another realm of life where all was colour and light.

Then he left and with his passing, so did all her hopes. She found no words for her lament, just a listless half-life, more listless than she had ever known. She believed that the world was darker for her than for any other creature. And yet, in the days to come she discovered that something still lived inside her. She did not quite recognize it. It was something light, something to do with a determination to live a full life, a longing to find true friendship and a love that would last. It was a longing that had survived the cold frosts of lament and had perhaps not only survived but even been strengthened by it. Her longing was part of her healing, and she found new energy. She discovered determination. She would be restless until she found what she so desired, but she could live with that restlessness and would allow herself to long, even if the longing was enduring.

This week we shall focus on the experience of longing. Humans have a remarkable capacity to long for that which they can't see. It is risky because it can end in disappointment and lament, but it is a risk worth taking. It can lead us on all kinds of adventures and explorations. A sense of 'there must be more to life than this' has caused people to change jobs, take up hobbies, visit new countries, emigrate, join political parties or give themselves to particular causes. For those with faith, longing can be a strong stirring in their spirit that motivates and energizes them to make the world a better place. Then there is the ultimate longing—the longing that yearns for a life beyond death.

For Christians this is a longing for heaven, which is closely connected with the longing for Christ's return to this world. The longer I live the more I long that this world becomes a better place, the more I long for God to answer our prayers, and the louder I want to sing at the Advent time of year when the darkness of winter has returned, 'Come thou long expected Jesus, born to set thy people free; from our fears and sins release us, let us find our rest in thee'[9] Who doesn't want to be free from their fears? Who doesn't want to be released from those parts of their character that damage others? Who doesn't want to find true resting places in this restless world?

Of course we sing with longing words like these: 'Come on Jesus, oh come on, we've been expecting you, yearning for you, desperate for you to come and heal, and change and transform my damaged life and this broken world.' Because a deep instinct within us needs to be reassured that it will all end 'happily ever after', we also long for some assurance that after this world, however it ends, there will be a world of peace, justice and sheer and utter joy, with no shadow of lament. Wherever we are on our journey of faith, there is sure to be part of us that yearns to know that heaven exists and pricks up our ears at those beautiful Bible passages that describe the new heaven and the new earth.[10]

Our longings are by no means pain-free; they are often birthed in the dark hours of lament and can feel quite fragile at times, but nonetheless they are extraordinary resources for the kind of hope that transforms our lives and the lives of those around us. This week we will meet some of those who knew such longings.

✛

8 December

The all-night wrestling match

The same night [Jacob] got up and took his two wives, his two maids, and his eleven children, and crossed the ford of the Jabbok. He took them and sent them across the stream, and likewise everything that he had. Jacob was left alone; and a man wrestled with him until daybreak. When the man saw that he did not prevail against Jacob, he struck him on the hip socket; and Jacob's hip was put out of joint as he wrestled with him. Then he said, 'Let me go, for the day is breaking.' But Jacob said, 'I will not let you go, unless you bless me.' So he said to him, 'What is your name?' And he said, 'Jacob.' Then the man said, 'You shall no longer be called Jacob, but Israel, for you have striven with God and with humans, and have prevailed.' Then Jacob asked him, 'Please tell me your name.' But he said, 'Why is it that you ask my name?' And there he blessed him.
GENESIS 32:22–29

Even by Genesis' standards, this is a pretty strange story. It is about Jacob, who is one of the many unlikely heroes in the Bible. Jacob's birth is described in Genesis 25 (vv. 21–26). His parents were Isaac and Rebekah, who had longed for children for many years and were delighted when they found out that Rebekah was pregnant. She discovered that she was carrying twins and her joy at carrying children was tempered somewhat by her awareness that they were fighting in the womb. She gave birth to two boys, and the first they called Esau, which means 'hairy' because he was covered in hair. The second they called Jacob, which literally means 'he grasps the heel', because that's what the baby was doing as he was born. Even at that stage he was grabbing hold of Esau, resenting his getting out first. The Hebrew for 'grasping the heel' carries the sense of 'deceiver', so these two boys found themselves bearing the names 'Hairy' and 'Deceiver', which must have raised a few laughs among their friends. Both of them lived up to their names: Esau was a gruff, rough man who loved hunting and the outdoor life; Jacob spent much of his time conniving with his mother about how to better himself, which resulted in his deceiving his father so that he robbed his brother of his birthright (vv. 27–34).

The years go by and the Genesis story centres largely on Jacob, but in chapter 32 we return to the conflict between Jacob and his brother. Jacob hears that Esau is on his way to meet him, and a messenger tells him that he is accompanied by 400 men (v. 6). Knowing the conflict that has existed between the two of them all their lives, and the way he has deceived him, Jacob understandably reads this as not just a family visit but a time to settle old scores. His imagination runs riot as he imagines a furious Esau, covered with hair and resentment, charging towards him and his family with 400 fighters. He plans all kinds of ways of pacifying his brother as well as strategies for protecting his family, which include sending his wives and sons and servants across the river. As he watches the wash from the carts and cattle, he starts to feel very alone on the shore. The writer puts it starkly: 'Jacob was left alone' (v. 24). His life of deceit has caught up with him; the people he loves are on the other side of the water, and on this side is one resentful brother with his 400 angry supporters.

I wonder what went through Jacob's mind in those moments— no doubt some regrets as he thought back through his life and realized with discomfort how much he had deceived not only his brother but others, too. I can imagine him, sitting in the moonlight, poking at the ground with a stick, assuming that this would be his last night on earth, restless with fear and feeling immensely alone. But then he discovers he is not alone: 'Jacob was left alone; and a man wrestled with him until daybreak' (v. 24). At this point of the story we don't know the identity of this wrestler, but we do know that they fight the whole night long, and Jacob musters up all his energy to grapple with this man. He was planning to fight his brother at dawn, but here he is fighting a stranger at night, and he is exhausting himself, so that when he meets his brother he will have no more fight left in him.

As the story progresses we realize that Jacob is not fighting a mortal, and in v. 30 he acknowledges that he has actually been engaged in a fight with God himself. At what point Jacob realizes this, we don't know, but it becomes clear that God has visited Jacob disguised as a man of similar strength to enact something that has been going on all Jacob's life. Jacob has lived a restless life, not at peace with himself, running away from closeness to God. Now he could not be any closer as he feels the muscles in the arms that hold him in a lock and smells the sweat of exertion and hears the grunts of stifled pain as he throws him in the dust by the dark river. It is God who eventually shows signs of tiring and so strikes a blow to Jacob's hip which heralds the end of the fight. It is God who says, 'Let me go, for the day is breaking' (v. 26), for this is a fight that can take place only at night. It is a fight that deals with the shadows in Jacob's life. Jacob, who is now aware that he has God in his grip, refuses to let him go until he is blessed. At last we get to the heart of the matter: Jacob got his human father's blessing by deceit, and his request here seems to indicate that he has never been confident of God's blessing. He may have imagined that he had deceived God as well—that all the good things that had happened in his life had been given by God because somehow God had believed Jacob's PR and spin. But here, in the sweat and dust of this wrestling match, he could not deceive God—God knows him for what he truly is, and part of what he truly is is a man who longs for God's approval. The question that is deepest in Jacob's heart has come to the surface, and it is the simple, age-old question: does God actually love *me*? It is a question that lies hidden in every human heart: 'If God really saw me, really knew who I am, knew what I think and do in secret, saw all the inner motives, all the foolishness and hurtfulness—that stuff that I have wrestled with all my life—if he really saw that, would he honestly want to bless me?'

The sun now comes up over the hill, and the two ragged wrestlers look at each other. Jacob is holding his hip which hurts, and he clenches his jaw, anxious no longer about his brother but about what his God thinks of him, and now he is waiting for an answer, not willing to let him go until he clears this up once and for all. 'Can you, will you bless me?' God answers, as he so often does, with a question: 'What is your name?' (v. 27). It is perhaps the one question Jacob dreads, for his name summarizes his character and his life story. He sighs and looks God in the eye and says, 'Deceiver', which is the name his mother gave him, and the name he has successfully lived by all his life. Until now he thought he might have deceived God. The question is, could Deceiver be blessed? And the answer is 'no'. Deceiver will not be blessed, because that is not who he truly is. 'Your name,' says God, 'is Israel,' which means 'one who has striven with God and humans and has prevailed' (v. 28). In my mind's eye, I can see a smile break out on God's face as he looks with delight on Israel. Remember Jacob's starting point: lonely and afraid because his brother was coming to fight him and he would be overwhelmed. His great fear was fighting and failing, but God calls him 'one who fights and prevails'.

With the confidence of one who is loved for who he is rather than for who he has pretended to be, Jacob (who is now Israel) asks his fellow-wrestler his name, and, as before, God replies with a question, 'Why is it that you ask me my name?' (v. 29). Israel gives no answer. Perhaps he is aware that this is a name he must discover for himself, and one he is actually well on his way to discovering. It is in that moment of the unanswered question that God does what Jacob has been longing for all his life—he blesses him.

The story is well known; it is simple; it is mysterious. It is the type of story that interests theologians and psychoanalysts alike. It is a story that reveals more meaning the more time you spend with it. It is a story that touches us for reasons we don't fully understand. But what we do grasp is that here is a man who longed to be loved and who came to a point in his life when he was lonely and afraid. Then he discovered a God who was willing to wrestle with his life with its struggles and questions, and who revealed his love for him, gave him his true name and blessed him. In our struggles to be loved, in the confusion we may feel about who we are, in our moments of loneliness and fear, it is good to know that we have a God who is more than ready to bless the person we really are.

Reflection

Take a moment to think about your name. Do you know what it means? Do you like it? Is there another name that you feel is more 'you'? If you were to meet God today, do you think he would bless the name you have, or bless you with another name?

Prayer

Lord, come and meet me in those places where I feel vulnerable and afraid. Help me to believe that you want to meet the real me, and when you do, despite the struggles in my life, please cover me with your blessing.

✛

9 December

Desperate for God

As a deer longs for flowing streams, so my soul longs for you, O God. My soul thirsts for God, for the living God. When shall I come and behold the face of God? My tears have been my food day and night, while people say to me continually, 'Where is your God?'

PSALM 42:1–3

This psalm should really be read in its entirety and also with Psalm 43, which is clearly linked to it. It is written by someone who is experiencing such a deep longing for God that they compare themselves to a deer searching for water in a parched land. Those of us living in the UK don't often witness this, but we see enough on our TV sets to know what drought looks like, even if we have never witnessed it first-hand. Most of us don't know what it is like to treasure every drop of water, or to know how bitterly painful it is to be desperate for water to drink. The psalm writer would know this from the experience of long, hot summers in the Middle East and the common sight of restless herds of deer roaming in search of a drink.

For this psalmist, the imagery of drought and thirst is used to describe how they are feeling about God. They write on behalf of the women and men who have known what it is to be close to God in their lives but who are now hitting a crisis. They have loved him deeply and served him as best they know how. They have witnessed evidence of his care and blessing in their daily lives, and when they come to worship they sing their hymns and say their prayers with a clear assurance that God is near and listens to them. Such a conviction of his presence is like a running stream for their souls, and spiritually they are refreshed. But for this writer, something has gone wrong. We don't know what has happened in their life, but some difficulty has occurred, so much so that cynics around are saying to them, 'So where is God then? He's clearly not much use to you now, just when you need him' (see v. 3). Such mockery simply adds to the tears that fall day and night. It is quite possible that this psalm is written by someone in exile, and the people around don't share the same faith as them, which only adds to the sense of loneliness and isolation.

If you read on in the psalm you find that this person is writing movingly and honestly about their longings. Verse 4 describes the painful nostalgia of remembering what it was like to go to the temple with other worshippers, singing and praying as part of a great procession with shouts of praise that erupted from the heart like gushing fountains of joy, in stark contrast to the dried-up riverbed that is their soul now. It is clear, however, that we are dealing here with someone who is not going to slump down in the dust of self-pity. They are looking for ways to get going again, to gain some momentum, some spiritual refreshment, even just a drop for their thirsty soul, and they ask themselves a question that feels to some extent like a reprimand: 'Why are you cast down, O my soul?' (v. 5). The rest of the psalm is a kind of argument, with part being an honest expression of longing for God to be close and alive, and the other part a response with reassuring words. The refrain that comes three times in these two psalms is 'hope in God', coupled with the conviction, 'for I shall again praise him, my help and my God' (vv. 5, 11 and 43:5).

There's no pietistic escapism in this psalm. It's rugged and real, written by someone who, despite the way life is currently treating them, is determined to find God again and who will not collude with the cynics around them. In the midst of the psalm there is a wonderful verse that reads,

By day the Lord commands his steadfast love, and at night his song is with me, a prayer to the God of my life (42:8).

Despite the thirst, the tears and the taunts, the writer goes back to one fixed point: the love of God, which is there by day, and at night is like a song that evokes prayer. The awareness of the love in the day and the song at night don't guarantee rivers of living water for the soul, but they do provide some hope to hang on to.

To long for God like a parched animal in a desert is not a concept that people easily understand today. We understand the world of human relationships, of people yearning for human love; we understand longings for freedom, longings for financial stability; longings to find a lost child. But you don't very often watch a soap opera in which one of the lead characters is in great distress because they just can't get close to God. Perhaps the nearest we get to this is when some tragedy takes place, and the age-old questions are asked as to why God didn't prevent it. But even that is hardly a longing for God—it's just not fashionable in our 21st-century western world. And yet, we look around and see such hurt and restlessness. All I need to do is to look at today's paper and I find evidence of this: there is the grief of a suicide bomber's wife; a person with a psychotic illness from smoking cannabis; a so-called celebrity accused of obtaining child porn and telling the court about how he was raped by a man when he was a child; a teenager shot dead on a London housing estate. I don't suppose any of the people featured in these stories would necessarily say they were longing for God, but is not some of our restlessness and dysfunctionality related to a deep longing for meaning in life, a thirst as real as that of the deer in the wilderness?

Psalm 42 speaks very much to those of us who have faith and who nevertheless have our moments when God seems remote and slow to respond. It offers us some important pointers for finding refreshment again. But the psalm is looking deep into the soul of all humans, and not just religious people. It probes into the heart of the distraught woman whose husband seemed so kind and gentle, and yet packed his bags with explosives and killed people in London on that July day, a day when she needed him most as she was in hospital losing their second child through miscarriage. She yearns more than ever to hear the songs of God in the night of her despair. It probes into the troubled mind of the person who in their confused state wishes so much that they had not partied with cannabis all those years ago, and tears are now their food day and night. It probes into the soul of the man known for comedy, now an image of tragedy in a London court as the waves of shame flood over him. It probes into every home on that housing estate where teenagers have been shot, and deep violence calls to deep violence in the roaring waterfalls of the unloved. All these life dramas slip back to an instinctive yearning for living water that heals, helps them to make sense of the chaos in which they find themselves and perhaps more than anything else gives hope. And, as I fold my newspaper on my lap and lean back into my chair, I connect once again with my hope and my longing that from time to time I will be allowed to hear songs springing up from the wreckage of our human tragedies.

Reflection

As you think about your life and the world in which you find yourself at the moment, where are the desert places? Spend some time pondering those places, and see what prayer rises up in response. Hold your prayer alongside the Psalmist's conviction: 'hope in God'.

Prayer

O Lord, when I am cast down and my soul is disquieted within me, lead me to that place where I can put my hope in you, that I may praise you, my help and my God.

❖

10 December

This is your land

He shall judge between the nations, and shall arbitrate for many peoples; they shall beat their swords into ploughshares, and their spears into pruning hooks; nation shall not lift up sword against nation, neither shall they learn war any more.

ISAIAH 2:4

The author of today's passage is a prophet who began his ministry in about 740BC when the king died (Isaiah 6:1). His name, Isaiah, means 'the Lord saves', and his message was fundamentally one of hope, yet much of the first part of his book rages at the people who pretend to be upright and religious but who have offended God in every conceivable way. Much of this early writing contains terrible prophecies of doom not only for Israel, but many other neighbouring nations as well.

He speaks into a world of turmoil where powers soar and fall. For those people who were not princes or prophets, much that happened around them was hard to understand, and they were often looking anxiously over their borders at the latest power to rise up and threaten them. All the time the people of Israel believed they were safe because God had promised them their land, but it was Isaiah's task to alert them to the fact that this promise was conditional on their living good and just lives that followed God's ways. Thus he begins his book with the word of the Lord admonishing the people who have rebelled (1:2), and then continues with predictions of the land becoming desolate with their cities burned and their fields laid waste by foreigners (v. 7). As the years go by, the land promised to Abraham by God (Genesis 15:7), inherited by the people who had been led by Moses across the desert for 40 years, and fought for by Joshua and his armies, became land that was besieged and eventually conquered. So the people who listened to these fearful prophecies of Isaiah were living in times of real uncertainty, longing for peace and security for their homes and families, yet aware that invading armies were never far away, and the hopes and dreams that sustained their ancestors were at great risk.

To read Isaiah's book you have to be prepared to be a time traveller: at one point you may be dealing with things to do with today, at the next you are being taken to the imminent fall of some great city; at another moment you are with the people of God in exile in Babylon; you also touch on the joyful return from exile, and there are moments when you are propelled to a period of time that is usually translated as 'the last days', a time when the world would be ruled by the Messiah with justice and peace. Thus, the chapter we are looking at today starts with a prophecy for Judah and Jerusalem in these 'last days' or 'the days to come' (Isaiah 2:1, 2). I find myself wondering what the people at the time understood by these prophecies of 'days to come'. No doubt the priests and prophets and theologians who were gathered around the temple took hold of these words and dissected them and considered them and had their theories but what about the shopkeepers and farmers, the teenagers and the young married couples? What did the 'normal' people make of all this, when they simply wanted a happy life that fulfilled their hopes of happiness and peace? No doubt on good days, when the world seemed relatively calm and peaceful, such prophecies felt rather irrelevant. So what, if in the last times swords would be beaten into ploughshares? So what, if nations no longer fight against each other? What's that got to do with us? Our lives are fine.

How different when life became insecure. When they heard the news that good friends had been killed by Assyrian raiders, they realized that the land that seemed so secure yesterday might not be theirs tomorrow. When they heard of homes being burned, they looked at the house built by their great-grandfather and knew that it might not be the home their children would inhabit. And as the skies grew dark with warfare and the grim prophecies of Isaiah started to come true, life became very fragile. In such times the long-term prophecies would have been called to mind: they might be the generation that would lose their land, their homes and their lives too soon, but they could at least hold on to one strand of hope: that one day, one of those 'last days', a moment would come when every last sword had been beaten into a ploughshare and every last spear was a pruning fork and the land that had been so drenched in human blood would be healed and inhabited by a people completely at peace and no longer needing to know about war. If they could hold that in their hearts, then they would have strength to face the present crisis.

We may consider such a notion naïve or escapist, but if we listen to the longings in our own hearts, we may well find something resonates with these 'last days' longings that we read about in Isaiah and other Bible passages. Many of us may be fortunate to live in lands which are very secure, where it is not hard to imagine that our children and grandchildren will live in peace. But every November as we approach the Advent season, we come to Remembrance Sunday and our minds are cast back to the conflicts of the last hundred years, in particular to the two World Wars. We go back in our mind's eyes to those terrible trenches of Flanders, the Somme and other places made infamous by dreadful conflict, and we think of young men being plucked from their normal lives and dying at the end of a bayonet in a field that had not long before been ploughed by peaceful farmers. We remember a world where there seemed to be no pruning forks or ploughshares but all seemed sword and spear. Twice in one century a land that had felt so secure was severely threatened.

That remarkable chaplain and poet from Worcester, Geoffrey Studdert Kennedy, witnessed first-hand the horrors of the trenches, and among his many lines that described so graphically the tragedy of war, he wrote,

Waste of Blood, and waste of Tears,
Waste of Youth's most precious years,
Waste of ways the Saints have trod,
Waste of Glory, Waste of God,—
War![11]

He wasn't afraid to admit his horror of war, but nonetheless he found a place of hope. In a booklet on his life, Michael Grundy gives a clue as to how 'Woodbine Willie' (as G. Studdert Kennedy was called) held together a deep honouring of those who had died and his hatred of war: 'I will love the things for which they died, and I will hate with a bitter lasting hatred the things that brought them to their death.'[12] In his view, those who had died did so in the belief that they were giving their lives for a better world, and Studdert Kennedy devoted the rest of his life trying to turn the church from an ambulance into an army. The work of this army was not destructive, but quite the opposite, as he demonstrated through his work for peace and social justice, exerting considerable influence in the UK and beyond.

Looking around at our world today, we are still very aware of the wars and the threats of wars around us. Those like Studdert Kennedy who lived so close to one of the worst wars in our history have helped us not only to find ways of expressing our horror of war, but also to find points of hope. After the war, his priority was taking the truly heroic qualities that he had encountered in humanity and applying them to efforts to change the world for the better. He longed for the church to become an army of peace and justice. Furthermore, he never lost his vision of the world to come, that world where there is no more war—no swords or spears. Such a world was not just wishful thinking. It inspired and energized his life and work in the here and now. He would have liked to have written poetry and songs describing such things, but in his moving poem 'The Unutterable Beauty' he realized that he was encountering a world that could not be described. Nonetheless, he knew such songs existed in the human heart, songs that connected with that deep intuition of a future land where there will be peace at the last. In his poem he prays that such songs may bring,

> *New light into the darkness of sad eyes,*
> *New tenderness to stay the stream of tears,*
> *New rainbows from the sunshine of surprise,*
> *To guide men down the years,*
> *Until they cross the last long bridge of sighs.*[13]

Reflection

What encounters have you had with war? Have you been to war and/or been close to someone who has? Do you fear war? What are your feelings as you think of this subject? What wars are you aware of today? What do you think about Studdert Kennedy's response to war?

Prayer

Lord, there are too many swords and spears in our troubled and restless world. Show me where I can be a warrior of peace, that with ploughshares and pruning hooks I may till the soil and tend the fruit of a land that is truly healed.

❖

11 December

Age-old questions

For I know that my Redeemer lives, and that at the last he will stand upon the earth; and after my skin has been thus destroyed, then in my flesh I shall see God, whom I shall see on my side, and my eyes shall behold, and not another. My heart faints within me!

JOB 19:25–27

Anyone who is on any kind of journey of faith, whatever their religion, will sooner or later come up against a major problem. The problem is expressed in many different ways but is essentially to do with the fact that if God is all-powerful and all-loving, then how is it that people who choose to follow him and obey his ways still go through hard times? Human suffering challenges the nature of God: if you are doing your best to follow God and obey his ways and you suffer, it is logical to conclude that God doesn't actually love you and therefore either doesn't care sufficiently to help you or doesn't mind treating you unjustly. Or you may conclude that God actually does love you very much and he is fair and just, but he just isn't able to help you—he would if he could, but he doesn't have enough power to assist and rescue you.

For Christians this is tricky, because we profoundly believe that God is love (1 John 4:8) and we believe he is all-powerful (Psalm 62:11). Suffering for a believer therefore has an added dimension of difficulty because we are not only going through the hard time, but we are also living with the question, 'Why isn't God helping me?' What usually happens in times like this is that friends come along and try to analyse the problem and work out what God may be doing, and although they may be well-meaning, the explanations can often seem somewhat forced and unconvincing. This is a particularly live issue when people become seriously ill. We know from our reading of the Bible and from Christian experience that God heals, and yet, despite our prayers and pleadings there are times when good and faithful people do not receive the cure we long for. Why is it that God appears to offer some people miraculous cures but not others?[14]

It is comforting to know that this problem has been faced by faithful believers for thousands of years, and the book of Job is the book of the Bible that faces this problem head-on. Before you get excited, it doesn't offer an easy answer to the problem of suffering! At the very least, though, it does offer us some companionship, and many are the people who have travelled with Job on a difficult road of suffering and taken comfort from his insights. We don't know who Job was, whether he was an actual person or fictional, or when he was supposed to have lived. All we know is that he was once a very successful, wealthy, honest family man who lived in the land of Uz, an area which lies to the east of the Jordan (Job 1:1). In the book of Job we meet a man who is hit by a series of devastating personal disasters and is also visited by a group of well-meaning but generally unhelpful friends who try to work out what God is doing in his life.

If you make your way through the book of Job, you will read the brief account of his suffering and then lengthy arguments by himself and his friends. As you read this strange book of beautiful poetry, you feel for poor Job in his suffering, especially during the inquisition by his friends that must have brought him to breaking point. I think that is the stage he is reaching in today's passage. Here Job, worn down by his personal tragedies, his fundamental questions about God's behaviour towards him, and by his friends' examination, now reaches into the core of his soul and brings out an astonishing declaration of faith: 'I know my Redeemer lives, and that at the last he will stand upon the earth' (v. 25). Job is declaring that, despite all the questions they are asking about the nature of God, which might very easily also be about the existence of God, Job knows—he *knows* with his deepest instinct, a knowledge that is beyond the realm of human reason, a knowledge that is located in a place in his soul that cannot be analysed or investigated. He just knows that, no matter what, this God is a Redeemer who is very much alive, and he can redeem any situation regardless of how grim it might be.

What I love about these verses is the sheer earthiness of them. This is not a step up to a more heavenly realm, where Job is getting himself free of this world and this body, but quite the opposite. He proclaims that his Redeemer will stand upon the *earth* and that in Job's *flesh* he will see God. Through his suffering, Job is discovering another way of looking at life, which is very much engaged in this earth and his body. In my work I quite often find myself getting close to people who are going through hard times, and it is not uncommon to find them experiencing a Job-like period of questioning about exactly what God is like and what he is doing in their lives. But quite often there is a moment, usually right out of the blue and unrelated to anything in particular, when they have an instant of realization: that somehow or other this God is standing upon the earth of their lives which has been shaken so much by the events around them. That awareness, however small it may be, is often enough to make them say like Job, 'My heart faints within me' (v. 27). Another translation might be, 'My heart longs within me.' In other words, the very things that you might think were throwing the person further away from God are paradoxically causing them to yearn for him more. This seems to be what was happening to Job.

One person who has been coming regularly to our Soul Café is an elderly man called John. A few years ago John lost his sight in one eye and most of his sight in the other. I used to drive him home after Soul Café and enjoyed my chats with him on the way. One evening he was telling me that he had just returned from a walking holiday along the Cornish coastal path. The main problem, he told me, was that his carer was inclined to lag behind him as he strode down the winding paths! I was intrigued by the intense pleasure John had gained from this holiday, and because he was more than happy to talk about his blindness, I said to him, 'John, for most of us, the pleasure of a holiday like that would be in the views of the sea and the coastland. How did you enjoy it without your sight?' In reply, he leant back in the car seat and breathed in, and said, 'Oh Michael, I can't begin to describe it to you. I walk along that path and feel the turf under my feet rather than the hard pavements of the city; I hear the cry of the gulls overhead and the sound of the waves on the shore rather than the constant noise of traffic; I breathe in the salty fresh air, rather than the polluted air around my home. When I feel all that, I don't need my eyes.' He had learned, like poor old blind Gloucester in *King Lear*, to see the world 'feelingly' and he had learned in his flesh to see God in new ways.

On another occasion I asked John what he thought of our Soul Café. 'I love it,' he said. 'For 70 years I've sat in old pews, singing the same old hymns, hearing the same old readings and listening to boring sermons. I'm ready for something new!', and he laughed a mischievous laugh. I realized then that John was now starting to see so many things in a new light and his insights continue to be a gift to us all. Like Job, he knew there were no easy answers to his personal suffering, but, also like Job, he dug deep into his soul and found a treasure trove of insight and faith. His longing was not for answers, but for life in all its fullness.

Reflection

What do you do when you meet suffering in your own life or in the life of someone you love? What questions do you ask of your faith and of God? What answers emerge today as you consider this?

Prayer

Lord, sometimes I feel I know so little, especially when I see the suffering in your world, but please lead me by your Spirit to that place in my heart where I can say, 'I know that my Redeemer lives, and in my flesh, I shall see God.'

✣

12 December

Longing in lost places

Though the fig tree does not blossom, and no fruit is on the vines; though the produce of the olive fails and the fields yield no food; though the flock is cut off from the fold and there is no herd in the stalls, yet I will rejoice in the Lord; I will exult in the God of my salvation. God, the Lord, is my strength; he makes my feet like the feet of a deer, and makes me tread upon the heights.
HABAKKUK 3:17–19

Being a prophet in Habakkuk's day was not a barrel of laughs. In that depressing series of events leading up to the conquest of Jerusalem and the subsequent exile in Babylon, there was not a great deal to be cheerful about and there was certainly a fair bit to make people depressed. Prophets like Jeremiah were quick to point out the causes of the forthcoming judgment, and, not surprisingly, the people were not overly eager to hear messages about their being miserable offenders who were in urgent need of God's mercy. Despite the fact that being a prophet was not the best way to make friends and influence people, courageous individuals were called by God to declare just how dangerous the situation had become. And they often did this in fairly in-your-face kinds of ways and received rough treatment as a result.

Habakkuk is one of the prophets of these disturbing times, and we understand that he was stirred to prophetic activity around the time of the battle of Carchemish in 605BC when the great and mighty Egyptians were routed by the Babylonians, demonstrating just how powerful this foe was, and therefore just how vulnerable Jerusalem was. Habakkuk must have joined the crowds in prayer, pleading with God to deliver them from this terrible threat, and his book begins with a sense of weariness as he cries out to God, 'O Lord, how long shall I cry for help, and you will not listen' (1:2). The opening verses are full of 'how's and 'why's to a God who is allowing terrible things to happen. Habakkuk is the 'McEnroe prophet' who effectively cries 'you can't be serious' as he protests at a string of wrong judgments by the divine umpire.

At this point, Habakkuk is an intercessor. He speaks our word to God. He gives voice to our sense of bewilderment and articulates our disappointments. But the intercessor-prophet doesn't stay in this place of agonized protest. Our passage today joins him at the end of his book in which he has been journeying through a wide range of feelings. He reveals that he is immensely aware of the sheer powerfulness of God (for example 1:12–17). He is also very aware of the anger of God, and at the beginning of the final chapter he cries out, 'In wrath may you remember mercy' (3:2). It is the prayer of a man who is vulnerable and confused as he faces the fact that the world as he has known it is going to change beyond recognition, and many of the pillars that kept it stable for so long are collapsing. Yes, he knows that he and his people are to blame, but surely God's mercy is stronger than his wrath? Habakkuk is a real listener, and his listening takes him beyond glib and easy answers. Chapter 2 begins with the words, 'I will stand at my watchpost, and station myself on the ramparts; I will keep watch to see what he will say to me' (2:1) and ends with the words, 'The Lord is in his holy temple; let all the earth keep silence before him' (2:20).

It is in that moment of silence that he becomes aware of the still small voice that is heard beyond the earthquake, wind and fire. And his waiting and listening has taken him into a new perception, for in these final verses of his book he takes his prophetic word right into that state of vulnerability and hopelessness that he has seen in himself and in others. He speaks to those who are looking around and saying, 'What's the point—there's no blossom on the fig trees; the vines are empty; the olive crop's failed; the fields are barren; the flocks have wandered off' (see 3:17). Habakkuk might have joined them and said, 'Well, yes. It's curtains for us, but we can comfort ourselves that it'll work out at some undefined point in the future, and our descendants should be OK.'

Actually that would have provided some comfort, but Habakkuk is discovering that the very pain of the desperate situation has an extraordinary potential to be highly creative. So he declares a surprising message: 'Though this calamity is here, yet I'll rejoice' (see v. 18). This is nothing to do with purchasing an artificial 'give-thanks-in-all-circumstances' Christian smile! It's about making contact with that quality we see in those wonderful songs from the suffering places of the world. Think, for example, of that lilting township music from South Africa that seems to gather suffering and glory into one swaying, weeping, laughing song and enables our feelings of confusion, anger and sorrow to be transformed into praise.

Ben Okri writes in his poem 'An African Elegy':

> *Do you see the mystery of our pain?*
> *That we bear poverty*
> *And are able to sing and dream sweet things...*
> *That is why our music is so sweet.*
> *It makes the air remember.*
> *There are secret miracles at work*
> *That only Time will bring forth.*[15]

This kind of rejoicing is a secret miracle indeed. It is about putting our trembling hand in God's and allowing him to take us to the heights, and it is as we venture to the heights that we begin to see things from a very different perspective, and it is on those heights that hope becomes secure in our hearts, because we start seeing things very differently to how we normally view them.

A favourite film of mine is *The Shawshank Redemption*. It has a most unpromising setting in Shawshank Prison and takes place over many decades following the life of a wrongly accused city banker Andy Dufresne, who arrives at the prison in 1947. His good friend is

Red, played by Morgan Freeman, a man full of humour and wisdom, who provides narration for us at points during the film. At one point, Andy is working in the warden's office when he discovers some records. He takes one and puts it on the gramophone and decides to connect it to the prison yard speaker system. The music is a duet from Mozart's *Marriage of Figaro* and the camera pans around the yard as every prisoner stops what he is doing and looks up, captivated by the beauty of the music. Red narrates:

I have no idea to this day what those two Italian ladies were singing about. Truth is, I don't want to know. Some things are best left unsaid. I'd like to think they were singing about something so beautiful, it can't be expressed in words, and makes your heart ache because of it. I tell you, those voices soared higher and farther than anybody in a grey place dares to dream. It was like some beautiful bird flapped into our drab little cage and made those walls dissolve away, and for the briefest of moments, every last man in Shawshank felt free.[16]

No matter how troubled the times, how drab our lives, or how secure the prison we may find ourselves in, there is always the possibility of a shaft of hope breaking in and taking us by surprise. Such moments can be experiences of extraordinary vision.

Reflection

Think back over some of the difficult times in your life. Did you have moments of seeing things from a different perspective? What gave you a sense of hope?

Prayer

Lord God, you are my strength; you make my feet like the feet of a deer and make me tread upon the heights. Give me the eyes to see the view and the ears to hear the songs of hope.

✤

13 December

The Messiah

For a child has been born for us, a son given to us; authority rests upon his shoulders; and he is named Wonderful Counsellor, Mighty God, Everlasting Father, Prince of Peace.

ISAIAH 9:6

We have seen that Isaiah's message was one that included some severe judgments as well as some wonderful prophecies of hope. Within the prophecies of hope are several that predict the coming of the Messiah. Today's chapter begins with those wonderful words, 'The people who walked in darkness have seen a great light' (9:2), and builds up to the announcement of the birth of a child who will have great authority and will be a counsellor, God, Father and Prince. Christians have always understood these words to be predictions of the coming of the Messiah in the person of Jesus, and this passage is often used in carol services during the Advent and Christmas season.

It is perhaps hard for us to understand what it means to long for the Messiah. It has always been a vital part of Jewish spirituality and is to do with a longing, an expectation that God will, one day, send someone who will put things right. In the Old Testament the term 'Messiah' or 'Anointed One' is in fact only used twice (Daniel 9:25, 26), but there are a number of passages like ours today, which express clearly an expectation of someone coming to rescue a confused and fallen world. Isaiah actually refers us to the coming of a rescuer in several passages. Among these there is reference to the son of a virgin who will be called Immanuel (Isaiah 7:14), a shoot from the stump of Jesse who will bear the Spirit of God and who will help the poor and needy (11:1–16), and there are several passages predicting the coming of a servant who will suffer, most notably in chapters 52 and 53. It was not difficult for the Christian Church to look at the life, character and ministry of Jesus and make connections between such prophecies and him. Christians therefore believe that in the years before Christ, God was speaking to people who had ears to hear about the person he would send to be their helper and rescuer. Inevitably some heard and some chose not to hear, and some were prevented from hearing by those who felt threatened by the idea of a messiah. But running through the pages of the Old Testament there is an unmistakable strand of prophecy that was looking to the coming of this messianic figure.

For people whose lives are well off and safe, there may not appear to be a real need for a messiah. They are managing quite happily and in our Western world today it is not difficult to lead a fairly self-sufficient life. However, when the world becomes a lot more precarious, as it was for the people of God who were at first living with the threat of exile and then in the reality of it, this hope of a messiah fitted very much with a longing deep within them. What they were facing was the nitty-gritty of human anguish—families torn apart by war, loved ones lost because of the diseases brought about by poverty, financial ruin, oppressive rulers and more. The longing was not just for some distant action by a God issuing orders from heaven but more a desire to see God come and muck in with the lot of his humans. In the weeks to come as we read the nativity stories, we see this theme emerging.

Today's reading therefore looks forward eagerly to the coming of a child who will be wonderful, princely and God, but who is first and foremost a child born to *us*. He is *our* child, one of us, and this is what would make those early listeners light up. Here was a God who was going to get involved.

As we look across the world and see the kind of men and women who have been instrumental in changing the fortunes of others, it is often those who have worked among people rather than over them who have made the greatest difference. People like Nelson Mandela come to mind, and one of the reasons we admire him so much is that he was first and foremost one of the people. He came from a typical Xhosa village and experienced grief at a young age when he lost his father and was subsequently placed with a distinguished tribal family. Even as a child he felt the bitter pains of the poverty and indignity suffered because of the apartheid system. He worked hard at his studies and became a lawyer, but he used his training to be with his suffering people rather than distancing himself from them. He became a political activist and leader of the African National Congress and subsequently spent nearly three decades in prison for his struggle against apartheid. Nelson Mandela is clearly a man who has been driven throughout his life by a straightforward love of people, his country and justice. If he had been haughty and distant, the chances are he would have achieved far less. You could almost say that a child was given to South Africa, the government eventually rested on his shoulders and he became a father to his people. Humans know the value of this kind of thing and instinctively know it works. The descriptions of the Messiah that we read in Isaiah move us so much because in a world so often dominated by the rich, the famous and the powerful, there is something in us that longs for the humble and the authentic.

As we approach the Christmas stories, we need to become alert to that part of us that longs for this kind of messiah who is so different from many of the figures who fill the screens of our TVs and PCs. There are so many, both known and unknown, who would never want to be famous, who have caught something of this and have been among us, inspiring us and changing the world. We long for the Messiah when we find ourselves weary of the superficial leadership that we see too often in our world, and we dare to believe that God really has come to this world in a way that we love, not fear, and that he is still here among us with divine sleeves rolled up and hands that have become dirty from reaching out to the dark, stained places of this earth.

Reflection

Put the biblical teaching about the Messiah to one side for a moment: if you were to long for God to come to earth so you could see, hear and feel him, what would he/she look like, sound like, feel like? How does the God you long for compare to the one you have seen in your church (if you attend one)?

Prayer

God, you are who you are, and I have my longings of who I want you to be. Fill the gap between fact and longing, that we may find common ground for our friendship.

✛

The return of the king

For the Lord himself, with a cry of command, with the archangel's call and
with the sound of God's trumpet, will descend from heaven, and the dead
in Christ will rise first. Then we who are alive, who are left, will be caught
up in the clouds together with them to meet the Lord in the air; and so we
will be with the Lord forever. Therefore encourage one another with these
words.
1 THESSALONIANS 4:16–18

Advent is usually seen as the season of preparation before Christmas.
It lasts for four weeks, so for most people it is the season of intensive
shopping, baking and icing Christmas cakes, card-writing, office
parties, planning trips to families, attending carol services and
nativity plays and all the other activities associated with these cold
December days. But in churches, the focus is not just on preparing
for the festival that celebrates the coming of Jesus as a babe to
Bethlehem; it is a season for anticipating the return of Christ, whose
second coming will be in triumph and glory and usher in the end of
the world. You might therefore expect that the churches of the land
will be filled with excited Christians eagerly awaiting the return of
their Lord. This has not been my experience, however!

There are some problems associated with this second coming
business. For a start, no one seems to know what will really happen.
Theologians argue over the exact meaning of the texts. The word
used to describe the study of the last things is 'eschatology'. (I like
the preacher who said, 'Don't worry if you don't know what
'eschatology' is—it's not the end of the world.') There are many
experts in eschatology and an abundance of theories about how,

where and when Christ will return and whether, where and when the Christians will be 'raptured' (a belief that there will be a meeting with Christ in the sky). It is frankly easy to become cynical and conclude that it is all too difficult to understand, a far-off issue that has no direct relevance to our lives.

Let's start with our passage today. We find Paul writing to the Christians at Thessalonica, which was a bustling sea port that had become an important communication and trade centre in the Roman Empire. It was the largest city in Macedonia with a population of about 200,000. Paul's visit there is recorded in Acts 17:1–9. He and Silas got a fairly hostile reception and had to leave by night. However, they had long enough to plant a church that soon became a vibrant Christian community. We have two letters from Paul to the Thessalonians in the New Testament, and both refer to the second coming of Christ. Every chapter of the first letter ends with a reference to the return of Christ (1:9–10; 2:19–20; 3:13; 4:13–18; 5:23–24), which probably suggests that the Thessalonians had been asking lots of questions about this. Although the letter is sprinkled with references to the return of Christ, it is in chapter 4 that he gives special attention to it (vv. 13–18) and begins by discussing what happens to those who have 'fallen asleep', which is his term for the Christians who have died. Paul explains to the Thessalonians that when the Lord returns, those 'sleepers' in Christ will wake up, and there will be a grand reunion with those who are still alive 'in the clouds' and 'in the air' (v. 17). At this point I become nervous, and I thought I'd just check Google images on the return of Christ—and sure enough there is no shortage of images of a dazzling Jesus surrounded by angels and ghostly figures in front of a golden sunrise.

Somehow it is very hard to read this without starting to imagine Hollywood scenes and straying into fanciful theologies. Many Christians get stuck with a rather simplistic vision, some become obsessed with the details of the events, and others just put it all to one side because it is too complicated and difficult to fathom. I thank God that there are theologians and teachers who work hard to help us understand these matters, but in essence I find myself coming back to a basic truth. No matter what the details are, there is a clear message running through the Bible that one day this world as we know it will come to an end, and part of that ending will be the coming again of Jesus. The focus of our attention needs to be primarily not 'how' but 'who'.

Christmas introduces us to Jesus Christ, the central figure of the Gospels, foretold in the Old Testament by the prophets. Thanks to Matthew, Mark, Luke and John we can read reports of his teaching and his deeds. Paul and the other New Testament letter writers help us to understand more of his teaching. Luke in his work 'The Acts of the Apostles' tells us what happened when people started to share the stories of Jesus and how it became evident that they were not just sharing a set of beliefs but introducing people to a God who was alive and very much on their side, who did wonderful things in their lives and gave them a hope for the future. For centuries after these pages about Jesus were written, people have continued to encounter him in all kinds of ways and have discovered him to be very real. I am one of them, and even though my knowledge still feels limited and my faith poor, I have discovered enough to know that more than anything else I want this world to be the kind of world that Jesus would make it. The more I read about Jesus, the more I find myself longing that he would be more present in my life, more present in this world, more present in aching Iraq, more present in the chaos of our inner cities, more present in the void left in the lives of those who have lost loved ones, those facing pain, sorrow and sickness of every kind. The feeling I have within me feels like a kind of homesickness, for the world to become truly the home that it was always meant to be—safe. This feeling brings to mind a well-known book.

I read J.R.R. Tolkien's *The Lord of the Rings* when I was a student at university. I was introduced to it by Tony, a friend who was doing Medieval Studies and knew the book intimately from cover to cover. If I was to engage in any meaningful friendship with Tony, I had to read the book that he was forever quoting to me. I remember clearly how the book completely took hold of me one Easter holiday and I spent two weeks completely engrossed in it—it was as if I was travelling with those hobbits on their fearful journey to Mount Doom. The book gets darker and darker as the power of Sauron grows, and as Sam and Frodo get nearer to Mordor. I found myself longing for them to be free, longing for Aragorn and his troops to be successful, longing for peace, order and goodness to return to this orc-infested world. Seeing Peter Jackson's trilogy of films brought back the same feelings, evoked the same longings. Watching the films again recently I found myself mentally pausing in admiration at Sam at that moment in Osgiliath where Frodo is dreadfully burdened with his call to carry the ring, and Sam gives his friend renewed strength by a great speech:

'I can't do this, Sam,' said Frodo.

'I know. It's all wrong. By rights we shouldn't even be here. But we are. It's like in the great stories, Mr. Frodo. The ones that really mattered. Full of darkness and danger, they were. And sometimes you didn't want to know the end. Because how could the end be happy? How could the world go back to the way it was when so much bad had happened? But in the end, it's only a passing thing, this shadow. Even darkness must pass. A new day will come. And when the sun shines it will shine out the clearer. Those were the stories that stayed with you. That meant something, even if you were too small to understand why. But I think, Mr. Frodo, I do understand. I know now. Folk in those stories had lots of chances of turning back, only they didn't. They kept going. Because they were holding on to something.'

'What are we holding on to, Sam?'

'That there's some good in this world, Mr. Frodo... and it's worth fighting for.'[17]

Reading the stories of Jesus in the Gospels reminds me of a world that truly is worth fighting for, and it is one that is called the Kingdom of God. Like Sam, we carry in our hearts a conviction that there will come a day when the king will return. We may not know the details of how or when, but we know it will happen and so we will keep going and our longings will strengthen us for the journey.

Reflection

What do you feel about the return of Christ? How relevant is the hope of his return to your life? What difference does it make to you today?

Prayer

Saviour, take the power and glory;
claim the kingdom for thine own:
Alleluia! alleluia! alleluia!
Thou shalt reign, and thou alone.[18]

Annunciation

We now come to the very well-known stories of the infancy of Jesus. On the day of writing this I have been to a nativity play in a local junior school. There I sat in a crowd of proud parents and assorted relatives as we watched a procession of narrators, singers, sheep, angels, donkeys, oxen and wise men gather around the characters of Mary and Joseph. The play centred on a rather cross sheep whose mood was changed by its encounter with the events of the nativity. No one needed to explain that ancient story—we all knew it. The story of Mary and Joseph and the birth of their son in a stable in Bethlehem is probably the best-known bit of the Bible. Despite the process of secularization, the vast force of Christmas commercialism and the attempts to replace 'Christmas' with more politically correct winter festivals, the story of that little family nonetheless endures like an indelible mark and is there in our schools and churches, on TV and radio, and on our Christmas cards. The words of the stories, enshrined in well-known carols, are played in shopping precincts and cafés. In fact, you would have to be incredibly unobservant if you got through Christmas without hearing something of Mary, Joseph and Jesus.

Of course, the problem is that the story can be treated like a much-loved fairy tale. It can be another Cinderella or Sleeping Beauty—a touching tale that has been told through the ages and brings us comfort and warmth. However, in the coming weeks we shall see that the birth of Jesus is anything but a fairy tale. It is a remarkable testimony of love, devotion, courage and honour. It introduces us to Jesus, who is claimed to be the Messiah, the Saviour, the God-with-us. We shall spend most of these days looking at the stories as related by Luke and Matthew, but we shall also look at John, whose Gospel was written a long time after the others.

Our readings this week will be from the first chapter of Luke's Gospel, in which he weaves together two extraordinary infancy stories. The central characters are Elizabeth and Mary, who each conceive their children in remarkable ways, and we shall see how in their response they demonstrate most impressively the way of hope.

15 December

The painful question

In the days of King Herod of Judea, there was a priest named Zechariah, who belonged to the priestly order of Abijah. His wife was a descendant of Aaron, and her name was Elizabeth. Both of them were righteous before God, living blamelessly according to all the commandments and regulations of the Lord. But they had no children, because Elizabeth was barren, and both were getting on in years. Once when he was serving as priest before God and his section was on duty, he was chosen by lot, according to the custom of the priesthood, to enter the sanctuary of the Lord and offer incense. Now at the time of the incense offering, the whole assembly of the people was praying outside.

LUKE 1:5–10

Luke begins his Gospel with a short introduction addressed to Theophilus, the recipient of his book, and then gets into his opening story, which is about an old couple called Zechariah and Elizabeth who are living in the days of King Herod in the Rome-conquered land of Judea. There was a succession of Herods who governed in those days. This one was known as 'Herod the Great', a Jew by birth who, by colluding with the Romans, gained great political power in the region. He was determined to make a name for himself and so engaged in many building projects, including a lavish palace for himself in Jerusalem and the reconstruction of the sacred temple. But his Jewish subjects hated him, partly because he collaborated with the Romans, partly because they did not view him as the rightful ruler, and partly because he showed scant regard for sacred aspects of the Jewish religion and freely built temples for pagan deities. The people therefore felt very crushed both by the imperial power of Rome and by the local tyrant, Herod.

In the context of this depressing climate, the people tried as best they could to make life bearable, and the priests had an important duty to keep faith and hope alive. One important characteristic of the priests was that they had authority entrusted not by some alien power or corrupt ruler, but through God and through long centuries of history. Every priest of that day could trace their ancestry back to Aaron, the brother of Moses, the greatest of all their leaders. On a day when the weather was bad, the Romans had been cruel and life seemed very tough, you could at least meet a priest and make contact with the line that went right back to the roots of your faith and remind you that the God who rescued his people time and time again was still around and was there to give you courage to press on. So the priests faithfully performed their duties and kept faith alive in their communities. One such priest was Zechariah. He was married to Elizabeth who, Luke tells us, was also a descendent of Aaron.

Zechariah was one of thousands of priests, and these priests were divided into 24 sections. In a very methodical way it was worked out when the various sections would serve at the great Temple in Jerusalem. When a section was on duty, the various tasks were divided up and given out by lot. All the duties were considered a great honour, but the one the priests most hoped for was to burn the incense on the altar. This duty took you right to the heart of the temple: you were entrusted to go as close to God as was considered humanly possible in those days. You lit the incense, and watched the smoke rise up, a symbol of the prayers of the people—the routine prayers of faithful religious people; the well-articulated prayers of the clever people; the rough-hewn prayers of the desperate people. Up to heaven went the prayers of the poor and the rich, the old and the young, the strong in faith and the weak in faith. The priest would gather those prayers in the cloud of incense smoke and bless them on their way to heaven, hoping and longing for divine favour.

If any of us had been the priest on duty, we would almost certainly be gathering into that cloud of prayer our own deepest prayers. I feel sure this would have been true of Zechariah. We really know very little of him and Elizabeth, but what we do know is that they carry a human story that is full of pain and sorrow. They had been unable to have children, and they had now reached the stage in life where Elizabeth had moved beyond child-bearing age. It is a hard burden in any culture, but it would have been particularly hard for a priest in the culture of that day. The rabbis taught that those who were unable to have children were excommunicated from God. If a woman could not bear children (and it was always deemed to be the wife's problem in those days), the husband had grounds for divorce. It seems harsh and cruel to our way of thinking, but sadly it is a conviction that has been present in many parts of the world over the centuries.

In the light of this, poor old Zechariah would have been on the one hand thrilled at the thought of entering this holy place with his request, yet at the same time burdened with the thought that when he got there, if the rabbis were right, he would meet with a disapproving divine frown. His childlessness would be a barrier; he would not be able to communicate with the one from whom he so desperately wanted help.

Straight away in his Gospel Luke introduces us to one of the great religious conundrums and one of the great religious deceits. The conundrum is the problem of innocent suffering. Luke tells us that Zechariah and Elizabeth were both direct descendents of Aaron. You could not have a better spiritual heritage than that. Not only that, but in verse 6 Luke tells us that both of them were, in the translation we have, 'righteous', a word that infers that they did everything correctly—they followed the religious laws as best they knew how, and Luke emphasizes this by telling us in the same verse that they lived blamelessly and followed all the commandments and regulations correctly. We are meant to understand that these are two very good people. Then in verse 7 Luke adds the 'But...' They lived this apparently perfect life, but something terrible happened to them. Here is the conundrum about innocent people's suffering.

Luke's 'but' here shows that he, too, understands this deep human and often religious instinct that says that if you live well, then things will go well for you, but if you live badly, bad things will happen. Zechariah and Elizabeth have lived well, and yet something bad has happened, so people conclude that either they have secretly done something wrong, or that something has gone wrong with God.

If that is the conundrum, the deceit is the view that the way to get close to God is to impress him. What unfolds in the pages of the Gospels and the other writings of the New Testament is a theme of grace as opposed to law. The God we see revealed in the Gospels is not a distant magistrate meting out punishments to the wicked and sending prizes to the good. The story that unfolds tells us of a God who is so much on the side of humans that he is willing to come and be among them. In our story Zechariah and Elizabeth are just about to discover the dimensions of this grace. They will discover that God has been deeply involved in their pain, not distantly judging them for it. They will discover that their righteous way of living has not been the way to impress God. He has been impressed with them simply because they are his beloved children.

Wherever we are on our faith journey, we will almost certainly have moments when the questions facing us seem beyond us. It is comforting to know that 2000 years ago there were people who also struggled with these questions. The German poet Rainer Maria Rilke wrote:

Be patient toward all that is unsolved in your heart and try to love the questions themselves *like locked rooms and like books that are written in a very foreign tongue. Do not now seek the answers, which cannot be given you because you would not be able to live them. And the point is, to live everything.* Live *the questions now. Perhaps you will then gradually, without noticing it, live along some distant day into the answer.*[19]

Zechariah was about to start living into an answer.

Reflection

What is unresolved in your heart? How have you been able to live with the questions? Can you look back at your life and see times when you lived with an unresolved question and then, after some time, you discovered the answer? What did you need to help you journey towards that answer?

Prayer

Lord, I come to the altar of your presence bearing the incense of my prayer. I have no fine words to offer, and no great works with which to impress you. I come nonetheless as a child with more questions than answers, asking that in the time between the question and the answer you will help me to find fullness of life.

✣

16 December

A surprising response

Then there appeared to him an angel of the Lord, standing at the right side of the altar of incense. When Zechariah saw him, he was terrified; and fear overwhelmed him. But the angel said to him, 'Do not be afraid, Zechariah, for your prayer has been heard. Your wife Elizabeth will bear you a son, and you will name him John. You will have joy and gladness, and many will rejoice at his birth, for he will be great in the sight of the Lord. He must never drink wine or strong drink; even before his birth he will be filled with the Holy Spirit. He will turn many of the people of Israel to the Lord their God. With the spirit and power of Elijah he will go before him, to turn the hearts of parents to their children, and the disobedient to the wisdom of the righteous, to make ready a people prepared for the Lord.'
LUKE 1:11–17

Yesterday we left an excited yet nervous Zechariah in the temple, offering the incense to God. Within the prayers offered on behalf of the people he almost certainly offers his own prayers to do with his sense of loss because he and Elizabeth could not have children. We now come to the first of several angel stories. Opinions and beliefs about angels vary greatly and I am not going to develop these now. The fact is that angels feature in many different religious traditions and nowadays there is a revived interest in them. In the Bible they visit humans on occasions to bring special messages (Genesis 16:7), they are known to defend those in times of trouble (Psalm 34:7), and in visions of heaven, angels can be seen worshipping God (Isaiah 6:2). Luke tells us (1:19) that the angel who appears to Zechariah is Gabriel, who is one of the two named angels in the Bible (the other is Michael).

I think we can assume that Zechariah was a fairly orthodox Jewish believer of his time who would have accepted the existence of angels. It probably never occurred to him, however, that he would ever actually meet one, even during such a sacred act as doing his priestly duty in the temple, as demonstrated by his sense of shock and terror when he saw Gabriel.

Angels in the Bible are accustomed to meeting terrified humans (the shepherds on the hillside in Luke 2:10 also needed to be told not to be afraid). I think most of us would be scared by such a supernatural encounter. It could feel very spooky. Not only that, there would almost certainly be a very strong atmosphere of holiness about an angel, and the bright light of its goodness would make us very aware of our many shortcomings. Following on from fear could well be a sense of shame. This was probably the case for Zechariah, and he would have felt very vulnerable.

The angel in this story does not just appear, he also speaks. He has come with a message for the startled Zechariah. I wonder what Zechariah thought Gabriel would want to say to him. This angel had come direct from the presence of God (1:19) and therefore whatever message he had would be of supreme importance. No doubt in the many prayers of the people drifting up to heaven in that cloud of incense there was the normal human mix of the trivial and the profound. There would have been prayers for God to bless those about to be married, those dying, those giving birth; there would have been prayers for the sick, for the poor and the lost. There would have been prayers for God to deliver his people from the burdens of Roman rule and Herod's malevolence. I think if I had been Zechariah at that moment, and I knew the angel was bringing a message, I would have assumed that someone outside had prayed an immense prayer that had mightily impressed God, and I was to be the delivery boy to take the answer to them. I would therefore have been utterly amazed when the angel said, '*your* prayer has been heard'. He had come to give Zechariah a personal message about his circumstances.

In case Zechariah is in any doubt, the angel goes on to make very clear which prayer has been heard: 'Your wife Elizabeth will bear a son' (v. 13). It is what Zechariah has longed to hear for years, perhaps 30 years or more. What intensity of excitement must have been in his heart when he heard this news! His wife *would* conceive. The angel doesn't stop there. He now gives some very specific information. Elizabeth is going to bear a son, and Zechariah is going to name him 'John'. At that point Zechariah would have started to form a little nagging question at the back of his mind, as the expectation would be that the baby would be named after the father (see v. 59). Gabriel then goes on to talk about the joy that the child would bring not just to his parents but to many.

There is then a rush of prophetic insight into John's future life, which must have been more than old Zechariah could really take in. In that incense-filled chamber, he listened with awe as Gabriel described the shape of his son's ministry: he would never drink alcohol; he would be filled with the Spirit even from birth; he would have the same power as Elijah; he would bring reconciliation between parents and children, bring back those who have strayed and build up a gathering of people who will be prepared for the Messiah.

In the first moments of this encounter Zechariah is amazed and delighted to discover that the message from the angel is so personal and is in response to his heart's yearning. Then, incredibly, he discovers the answer is not simply a domestic issue. The way the angel is answering his prayer is to send him not just any child, but a child who is going to be another Elijah and who will prepare the way for the Messiah! By any reckoning this is an astonishing piece of news. One moment Zechariah is just an ordinary man with a very human need and the next he is being told he will father one of the greatest religious figures ever.

Perhaps what this tells us is that praying for something carries certain dangers! We all have our yearnings and longings, and these often find their way into our prayers, crying out to God to help us, rescue us, provide for us. What this story tells us is that God is listening. He is not a slot-machine God—put the right coins in, pull the lever and you get the prize. No, God's way of working in our lives is far more personal. There certainly are times when he does answer prayer dramatically. As Zechariah discovered, sometimes the answer is not quite what he was expecting. It was certainly personal, but this answered prayer was going to help not just Zechariah, but a whole community of people.

Maybe this is a clue as to how God answers our prayers. Perhaps today's story shows us that God certainly listens to every prayer we ask and compassionately understands the longing of our hearts. Yet he also always sees us in the context of the human communities in which he has placed us. You may ask for something personal, but the answer may well be for the benefit not just of you, but of the community in which you live, work or worship. A distinctive feature of God's gifts is that they are for sharing.

Reflection

What are some of the prayers deepest in your heart today? Imagine if God were to send you an angel—what do you think he would say to you? Can you think of an answer to your prayer that would be not just for you but for the community of people around you?

Prayer

Lord, you know the longings of my heart, and once again I offer these to you today. Make me open to your response, however surprising it may be, and give me a generous spirit that I may freely share what I am given.

17 December

Lost for words

Zechariah said to the angel, 'How will I know that this is so? For I am an old man, and my wife is getting on in years.' The angel replied, 'I am Gabriel. I stand in the presence of God, and I have been sent to speak to you and to bring you this good news. But now, because you did not believe my words, which will be fulfilled in their time, you will become mute, unable to speak, until the day these things occur.' Meanwhile, the people were waiting for Zechariah, and wondered at his delay in the sanctuary. When he did come out, he could not speak to them, and they realized that he had seen a vision in the sanctuary. He kept motioning to them and remained unable to speak. When his time of service was ended, he went to his home. After those days his wife Elizabeth conceived, and for five months she remained in seclusion. She said, 'This is what the Lord has done for me when he looked favourably on me and took away the disgrace I have endured among my people.'
LUKE 1:18–25

Zechariah listens in some amazement to the angel's description of his son who is soon to be conceived. Despite the dramatic vision of an angel, Zechariah still harbours a seed of doubt. Recovering a little from the shock of seeing an angel, he now seems to feel secure enough to carry out a conversation. He has heard Gabriel's prophecy, but he needs to be sure about it, so he asks, 'How will I know that this is so?' His question is really very revealing. On the one hand the angel who stands in the presence of God has visited him in the temple sanctuary and told him that a miracle will take place. On the other hand, the fact is that Elizabeth is now well beyond child-bearing age and her conceiving is very unlikely, if not a medical impossibility. God has said that his wife will conceive; Zechariah's mind says that this is impossible. His mustard seed of doubt could destroy the mountain of hope that has just been given him. 'How will I *know*?' he asks this mighty angel. For him, an angel's promise is not enough. He needs more evidence, something factual, down-to-earth.

What is it that is troubling Zechariah here? Surely, even the most sceptical of us would not find it difficult to believe the most momentous miracle if it were delivered by an angel who spends his time in the presence of God? It's only one short step of having a direct visitation from God himself, so how can Zechariah have trouble believing this? Perhaps he is bothered about convincing Elizabeth. You can imagine the conversation:

'Hello, darling, how did you get on in the temple?'

'Great. I drew the incense lot.'

'That must have been special.'

'It was. And, oh, er, an angel appeared to me.'

'Oh yes...?'

'Yes, the one that usually stands in the presence of God.'

'Mmm—that one? What sort of incense was it again?'

'And the angel gave me a message.'

'A message?'

'Yes, he said you would soon conceive and we would have a son and I would call him John and he will be like Elijah.'

The ensuing actions could then involve a broom and a bit of verbal abuse including several references to age. Zechariah may have been a priest, but he was also a normal human being, as was Elizabeth. I suspect he was very worried that no one would believe him, and he'd be left looking foolish and very alone with his remarkable piece of news. So he wants the angel to give him a hand, which the angel is not prepared to do. In fact, Gabriel is far from pleased by Zechariah's request. Zechariah's loss of nerve is not going to threaten the prophecy, but it will have consequences for Zechariah himself. He is to lose his power of speech. For Zechariah this must have been appalling—he had seen an angel and heard a wonderful message, but now he would have no way of telling people other than sign language and scribbles on tablets. If you have played games like charades, you'll know it is not easy to communicate without words.

All this interaction with the angel takes a while, and Zechariah is in the sanctuary for longer than normal. The crowd outside become inquisitive, wondering what has kept him. Eventually he appears and tries to explain what has happened. It must have been somewhat humorous to see him trying to mime this story of angels and babies. We get the impression that he failed to communicate the content of the message, although the crowd did realize that he had had a vision. Zechariah has to wait until his period of service has come to an end, and this must have given him much time to think and ponder on the angel's promise, and also time to think about how to tell Elizabeth.

When he finally gets home, he somehow manages to convey the message to Elizabeth and, sure enough, she does miraculously conceive. She decides to stay in seclusion, no doubt wanting to be careful about who heard this news. She wanted to ponder it in her heart, prepare herself for giving birth to a child who was going to be full of the Holy Spirit. Whatever was going on in her heart and mind, her predominant feeling, according to Luke, is one of gratitude (v. 25). God has shown his favour to her, and now the disgrace that she had felt for so long (because of that terrible culture of rejection by the community) has been taken away. In fact, she seems more delighted by that than by the baby she carries, which perhaps tells us just how painful the rejection had been for her.

This story depicts well the balance of faith and doubt we often find ourselves in. I get the impression that Zechariah had more or less come to the end of his longings. For years he had wanted a child and cared deeply for his wife, Elizabeth, who had had to endure that terrible sense of disgrace because of her infertility. At the end of his tether, he meets with God and remarkably God answers and gives him his heart's desire but in such a way that is far from comfortable. We don't know how Elizabeth responded to the news, but the impression we get of her is that she was a person of secure faith, able to accept that God could do remarkable things. It is Zechariah who wavers, and Elizabeth is steady. She knows that it is 'the Lord [who] has done [this] for me' (v. 25).

Most of us find the faith–doubt balance very difficult. We are required to believe without the normal evidences that make belief easier. If I am out walking and come to a wooden bridge across a stream I mentally go through a process, usually subconsciously, of weighing up whether the bridge looks secure. If I decide that it does, I happily walk across it. But faith is very different. We have to trust a God whom we can't see with our eyes or hear with our ears or touch with our hands or taste with our tongue. We have to draw on our spiritual senses that are quite different, yet related. Zechariah and Elizabeth got to know a God who not only existed but cared for the details of their lives and heard their yearnings. As far as we know, Elizabeth had not seen God nor his angel, but she was in no doubt that the reason she had been able to conceive in old age was because of the touch of God who loved her. And here perhaps is the clue. Faith comes not primarily from knowledge but from love. Zechariah and Elizabeth encountered God's love, and as a result they could believe.

A friend of mine was once chatting to his young son when he was putting him to bed. As was their custom they said their prayers. He then said, 'Adam, you have just spoken to God, but you can't see him. How do you know he's there?' Adam answered, 'Well, Dad, when you turn the light off, I can't see you, but I know when you are there.'

Reflection

When do you find it hard to have faith? What helps you to have faith? For what do you need faith today?

Prayer

Lord, I would like to grow in faith. Too often I am like Zechariah, hearing your word and then wanting more proof. Help me to trust you and, like that child in the dark, know you are there even though I can't see you.

✥

18 December

Highly favoured lady

In the sixth month the angel Gabriel was sent by God to a town in Galilee called Nazareth, to a virgin engaged to a man whose name was Joseph, of the house of David. The virgin's name was Mary. And he came to her and said, 'Greetings, favoured one! The Lord is with you.' But she was much perplexed by his words and pondered what sort of greeting this might be. The angel said to her, 'Do not be afraid, Mary, for you have found favour with God. And now, you will conceive in your womb and bear a son, and you will name him Jesus. He will be great, and will be called the Son of the Most High, and the Lord God will give to him the throne of his ancestor David. He will reign over the house of Jacob forever, and of his kingdom there will be no end.'
LUKE 1:26–33

Yesterday's story left us with Elizabeth, five months pregnant, and rejoicing in the way God had blessed her. Today the story switches to another woman, who is going to be the second recipient of a dramatic piece of news conveyed by an angel. We come to the story of Mary who, according to Luke, is a relative of Elizabeth (v. 36) and they are therefore known to each other. If Elizabeth's story is about one who carries a child in old age, Mary's story is quite the opposite. It is commonly supposed that Mary was a teenager, as it was the custom for women to be betrothed at a young age. The scene is the small Galilean town of Nazareth—not a particularly distinguished town, and in fact held in derision by some (see John 1:46).

Here in this little town we find a young woman, Mary, who is betrothed to Joseph. Betrothal lasted for a year and was as binding as marriage. It was a declaration of intent and the couple were as good as married, though according to Jewish law there was to be no consummation until after marriage. Luke is writing to a non-Jewish readership, so he informs his readers that Mary is a virgin as he is preparing them for the immense miracle that he is about to describe. The setting is a very ordinary one: a young woman betrothed to a man in a small Galilean town. Then, once again, the story takes a dramatic turn with the arrival of an angel; in fact the same angel that appeared to Zechariah—Gabriel, who spends time in the presence of God and so knows well what is in God's mind.

It is tantalizing that we don't know anything of the circumstances of this meeting of Mary and Gabriel. Was it during the day or at night? Was it in her home, or when she was out walking in the fields? I suppose we don't need to know this, but it had to be at some time in the run of her normal everyday life, unlike in the previous story, where Gabriel turns up in a very holy place. Angels prove themselves to be comfortable anywhere in the world, no matter how religious or secular the place. So Gabriel makes a sudden appearance to Mary and greets her with the announcement that she is greatly favoured. It is very difficult to translate this word adequately. It is used only twice in the New Testament and indicates that the recipient is held in the highest possible esteem. The other place where this word is used is in Paul's letter to the Ephesians (1:6), and I'll return to that in a moment.

In Mary's case the use of this word is quite understandable. She has been selected by God to bear his only Son. As he did with Zechariah, Gabriel now tells Mary about this child she is to bear. Firstly, his name is to be Jesus. Luke makes no comment on this, for this is a Gentile name and is familiar to Luke, who came from the Gentile world. For the Gospel writer Matthew, however, there is something unusual about this name, and he makes sure the reader understands the reason for it (Matthew 1:21). Hebrew-speaking Jews would have expected a Jewish name, and the Hebrew equivalent of Jesus is Joshua, which means 'the Lord saves'. By giving him the name 'Jesus' the angel is giving two clues about the nature of his life: the first is that he will be involved in some activity involving saving people, and the second is that he will have an influence beyond the circle of Hebrew-speaking Jews. Gabriel expands on the ministry Jesus is to have and tells Mary that he will be 'great, and will be called the Son of the Most High, and the Lord God will give to him the throne of his ancestor David. He will reign over the house of Jacob forever, and of his kingdom there will be no end' (Luke 1:32–33).

It is impossible to know how Mary felt at this point. One moment she is having a normal day or night, and the next there is an immensely important angel speaking to her, telling her that she is going to bear a child who will be a king in the line of David, and not a normal king at that, but one who will rule a kingdom that will never come to an end. In this announcement there is already a prediction of Jesus' resurrection. He will not be a king who will come and go—his reign will survive beyond death and therefore his kingdom is going to be uniquely different from anything else the world has experienced. At the same time, there are some familiar landmarks given with the names of Jacob and David.

Tomorrow we shall see how Mary responds to this astonishing news. For today, let's pause at the moment when the angel arrives and calls Mary 'favoured one', that rare and unusual word. Few would doubt that it would be appropriate to use it for Mary, who had the unique task of carrying the Son of God. But in what other context might it be used? If we go to Paul's letter to the Ephesians, we find it used for others. Paul starts his letter by telling the Ephesian Christians how God sees them, now that they are 'in Christ'—that is, they have chosen to believe in Christ and place their lives in his hands. In the middle of quite a complicated bit of theology, Paul says that because of this they are 'accepted in the beloved' (Ephesians 1:6, KJV), which is the same as 'highly favoured'. In other words, God views them as he viewed Mary—with exceptional favour.

It may be quite hard for us to get our heads round this, and we may never catch up with the full implications of Paul's theology here, but the fact of the matter is that at the heart of the Christian faith is a God who, because of what Jesus is and has done, comes to us and greets us with the words 'you are immensely valued and favoured'.

This is a far cry from that parody of Christianity with a 'thou-shalt-not' God, always trying to spot secret sins and constantly disappointed by our feeble attempts to live a holy life. Yes, ours is a holy God, without a doubt. But we find in the unfolding story of the Gospels a God who is very much on our side, who is delighted to be with us, and whose love and mercy means that we *want* to live better lives, rather than driving ourselves to do better because of guilt.

As we shall see, Mary was shaken by this news, but never once did she argue with this angel or act bashful and suggest that he try someone more worthy. There was something about the way the angel brought this news and the openness of Mary's heart that helped her to know that her favoured status was a fact, not God's trying to win her over or butter her up with false praise. In short, she caught sight of the love that God had for her, and once she had seen this she became open to going on his adventures.

To step into the life of Christ means that we enter a world where we are loved extraordinarily by God. If we could only grasp that, we, too, would have the confidence to embark on the adventures God has for us.

Reflection

If an angel of God were to appear to you today, what do you honestly think he might say to you? (Don't look for a correct answer, but try to explore what is naturally in your heart.) Now take what you think and put it alongside the phrase in Ephesians 'accepted in the beloved', and allow it to seep into your heart and mind, and see what happens.

Prayer

Visit those bits of me, Lord, that hold a false view of you, and change them by the light and truth of your Holy Spirit. Help me to grasp the depth of love you have for me, so that I may have the courage to join you on whatever adventures you have in store for me.

✛

19 December

The overshadowing

Mary said to the angel, 'How can this be, since I am a virgin?' The angel said to her, 'The Holy Spirit will come upon you, and the power of the Most High will overshadow you; therefore the child to be born will be holy; he will be called Son of God. And now, your relative Elizabeth in her old age has also conceived a son; and this is the sixth month for her who was said to be barren. For nothing will be impossible with God.' Then Mary said, 'Here am I, the servant of the Lord; let it be with me according to your word.' Then the angel departed from her.

LUKE 1:34–38

If someone completely unacquainted with Christianity were to visit many churches across the world, judging from the statues and paintings they discover in those churches, they may conclude that Christians worship two gods: a man hanging on a cross and a woman dressed in blue, often to be found holding a baby. I wonder what conclusions they would draw about this religion. It's hard for those of us who know the Christian story and who have knowledge of the centuries of church disagreements about Mary to have any inkling about what might be going on in the mind of an outsider. But my guess is that such a person might actually be very impressed. From those statues and paintings of the crucified man they would know that this religion has a sympathy for suffering people; from the images of the young mother, they may well conclude that within this religion there is a gentleness, a loveliness and a high regard for the feminine and mother love.

Christians have much to be ashamed of as we look at the chequered history of our Church, but one of the things that saddens me most is the way Mary has been an object of argument between Roman Catholics and Protestants in particular. Traditionally both hold different views about her. In the New Testament, while she is much respected, there is no sense that she is particularly exalted above other human beings. As we saw yesterday, she is acclaimed 'highly favoured', but Paul declares that all in Christ are held in that esteem. The last mention of Mary in the Bible is in Acts 1:14, where she is part of a prayer meeting of the early Church, not leading it but simply happy to be there. However, as theologians explored what it meant for this woman to carry and give birth to the Son of God, they began to conclude that she must have been very exceptional. Thus doctrines developed of her 'immaculate conception' (that she was sinless from the moment she herself was conceived), her perpetual virginity (therefore she had no other children), and her 'corporeal assumption' (that is, she was so perfect that she did not die but went directly to heaven). I mention these matters in a space of a few lines, but in the history of the Church these three alone have been the subject of immense controversies, debates, anger, prejudices, divisions and even deaths. Both Catholics and Protestants have been as guilty as each other of using this beautiful character from the Bible as a focus for our disgraceful battles with each other.

Personally, I have always held a more Protestant view of Mary, but I love the way that Roman Catholic doctrines have placed such high regard and affection on Mary and I have learned much from them. As usual, I don't suppose any one wing of the Church has got it completely right, and what is important is meeting those of different views to help our understanding and prevent us from sliding into prejudice. Today, however, I want to elbow my way past the quarrels of the past and make my way back to that young woman in Nazareth who was on the one hand wonderfully ordinary and on the other quite extraordinary. The angel Gabriel is standing before her and calmly tells her that she is to bear God's Son, who will be the saviour of the world. Mary is impressively practical in her response. There is almost a hint here that she suspects the angel might have got the wrong person. Perhaps she feels that what the angel needs is a woman who is actually carrying a child or is at least married so that she can conceive soon. As far as Mary is concerned, the difficulty is that she has not had sex with a man, and she is not due to marry for some time, and therefore there is no way she can be with child soon. In response to this, the angel delivers the next bombshell. It's not that God is going to bless a child that she might carry—it is rather that God will be the father of the child. The Holy Spirit will enable the 'power of the Most High to overshadow' Mary (Luke 1:36). That word 'overshadow' (*episkiazo* in Greek) is a word that Luke, Matthew and Mark use for the moment in the story of the transfiguration, where Jesus is on the mountain with three of his disciples, and a cloud 'overshadows' them (9:34). Luke uses this word very carefully to convey the sense of something very mysterious indeed. It implies something big covering you and bringing a darkness—not making you darker, but making you aware of a blinding and wonderful light, too dazzling for your mortal eyes to behold. The darkness of the shadow speaks both of the intense mystery of this event but also of the existence of a most glorious light.

Mary is therefore to have this profound mystical experience. The reason for it happening this way, says the angel, is because the child is to be holy. Sadly, over the centuries, some have concluded from this that any natural conception involving intercourse would inevitably mean that a child is stained with sin right from the start, and some even taught that sex itself was sinful. But this is not how I read the passage. Gabriel is communicating something truly extraordinary to Mary: it is not that the holy God wants to *adopt* a human child and have it raised as his own; it is rather that he wants to come and join the human race as one of their own. To enable this to happen, he has chosen the role of father in the human process of reproduction, so that there is no question that the child who is born is not just human but divine as well. Millions of pages have been written over the years on this subject— the divinity and humanity of Christ—and it seems absurdly simplistic to summarize it like this. But I'm trying to think about that first encounter of the angel with Mary and what would have been going through her mind during the conversation. Her practical question about the fathering is given a practical answer by the angel, and as far as we can tell this is enough for Mary. She understands. She may be shocked and frightened, but she is aware of what is needed.

The angel knows of the immensity of this message and the burden it will lay on Mary's young shoulders, so he gives her a wonderful piece of practical help. There is an older woman who is also involved in these events. Mary can go and see her, so that she is not alone with her news. Her cousin Elizabeth is full of wisdom and will be a great support. The fact that Elizabeth is pregnant in her old age is another sign of the remarkable dimensions of God's power, which can overshadow humans and bring about extraordinary events. The angel's message is finished. Mary has no more immediate questions. She has understood what is required, and very simply responds by saying, 'Here am I, the servant of the Lord' (1:38). This reveals her wonderful attitude of humility: she just wants to serve her God as best she knows how. This cannot have been an easy 'yes'. It is a 'yes' of surrender, of letting go, of trusting the God of the impossible. She has moved from disturbance, through fear, to questioning, to listening to God's plan, to hearing of practical support, to saying 'yes'.

Any of us can feel at any time in our lives that too much is being asked of us, that we are too young or too old, that we don't know enough, that we don't have sufficient resources, that we are being asked to do the impossible. But here in these nativity stories, we find two women, Mary and Elizabeth, one young and one older, as two examples of faith and hope. And tomorrow we see what happens when they meet.

Reflection

What is your understanding of the significance of Mary? Have you been most influenced by Catholic or Protestant teaching about her, or none at all? What impresses you most about her? Is there a situation that you are facing in which you feel God is asking too much of you? Can you risk saying 'yes'?

Prayer

Holy Spirit of the Most High God, overshadow my heart and bring to birth new life, new hope and a new willingness in me to say 'yes' to you.

✣

20 December

Kindred spirits

In those days Mary set out and went with haste to a Judean town in the hill country, where she entered the house of Zechariah and greeted Elizabeth. When Elizabeth heard Mary's greeting, the child leaped in her womb. And Elizabeth was filled with the Holy Spirit and exclaimed with a loud cry, 'Blessed are you among women, and blessed is the fruit of your womb. And why has this happened to me, that the mother of my Lord comes to me? For as soon as I heard the sound of your greeting, the child in my womb leaped for joy. And blessed is she who believed that there would be a fulfilment of what was spoken to her by the Lord.'
LUKE 1:39–45

I like the inclusion of the words 'with haste' in this passage. We left Mary yesterday, having just heard the news, and she clearly can't wait to go and see Elizabeth. I assume that at this time Mary was still living in her parents' home. I wonder what she said to them? 'I'm just popping over to see cousin Elizabeth as I've got something to tell her.' Had she spoken to Joseph yet? The impression you get from the story was that she dashed to Elizabeth without telling anyone else, so keen was she to meet the one other person in the world who was involved in this extraordinary story.

There is immense energy and excitement in this passage. Mary is rushing to see Elizabeth; the child leaps in Elizabeth's womb; Elizabeth is filled with the Holy Spirit and is very vocal. Poor old Zechariah, who is still unable to speak, must have looked on with great astonishment! In writing this I did an Internet search to have a look at some of the paintings of this meeting between Mary and Elizabeth. There are many classical paintings, often depicting two rather serious women, very staid and saintly, clearly discoursing on very holy matters. I came across one, however, that really caught my attention. It is a painting by a Malaysian artist called Hanna Varghese, produced for the Asian Women's Resource Centre for Culture and Theology, which brings together women and women's organizations in Asia that are engaged in promoting Asian women's theology.

I recommend having a look at Hanna's painting on the website.[20] The painting uses bright oranges and blues and is full of sunlight, warmth and vitality. It captures beautifully the utter delight of these two women in carrying their special babies. Mary is depicted as having the freedom of a child, running down a hill and waving in delight, while the older Elizabeth lovingly opens her arms, sharing Mary's joy, but also offering the support that Mary needs. The painting also carries a forewarning as the angle of Mary's raised arms looks very like the angle of her son's in paintings of him on the cross. Her outstretched palms speak of her 'yes' to the angel, just as her son will give his 'yes' to the nails of the cross.

Mary must have been very relieved to meet Elizabeth, and we get a real sense that they were kindred spirits—two women of different ages, yet their lives and spirits entwined by the extraordinary events that had overtaken them. But the story is not just about these two: the child in Elizabeth's womb joins in. In recent years advances in medical technology have enabled us to see wonderful pictures of the child as he or she develops in the womb. We now have proof that even from the earliest weeks, babies have significant awareness of the outside world, which increases as the pregnancy progresses. At six months they are certainly aware of their mother's moods; they recognize different voices and respond to music. Luke, who has traditionally been identified as a doctor, was possibly aware of this and has certainly no difficulty in reporting that the unborn John the Baptist joined in his mother's celebration. We are also given to understand that it was not simply a matter of John's picking up the joy felt by his mother, but that in fact it was John who detected the good news first. This unborn child had a sharp intuition that sensed the nearness of Mary and of the unborn Son of God in her womb. True, we know that John was particularly gifted by the Spirit, but nonetheless there is a sense here that even unborn children may have the capacity to sense and detect the presence and activity of God and respond with praise.

When Luke is writing these stories, he is often keen to point out the activity of the Holy Spirit. The arrival of Mary and the leaping of the baby in her womb is for Elizabeth accompanied by an experience of being filled with the Holy Spirit, so that she gives a shout of praise, unrestrained and delightfully free. Anyone who thinks that Christianity is about sober good behaviour and fine manners needs to think twice when reading this story! To use Charles Wesley's words, the joy of heaven to earth has come down—and the earth knows about it![21]

In these verses, Elizabeth's delight is expressed in a typical mix of exclamation and question. At first she praises Mary and declares that she is blessed among women, and the child of her womb is also greatly blessed. Then she is so overwhelmed by the magnitude of this that she suddenly feels very humbled and asks why such a great mother and baby should come to visit her. She knows they are so significant because the special prophetic baby in her womb testifies by leaping inside her (which can't have been hugely comfortable!) Then, after her question, she again praises Mary for believing what God had said to her, even though the message had seemed utterly improbable.

Here we see two women responding in a wonderful burst of joy to the good news. The reason why Mary and Elizabeth were so full of joy was not just the normal delight of women who were privileged to carry children; it is clear that theirs is a deep spiritual joy to do with hearing God and deciding to trust what he says and believe his promises. The normal pressures of life can sometimes cause us to live a kind of half-life, where we forget to listen to God and choose the way of cynicism instead of the way of faith. As a result we may find ourselves denied the running, shouting, leaping joy that is part of the God-given repertoire of human experience. If we dare to take the risk, listen to God and open ourselves to believing what he is saying, then who knows what sparks of true joy might catch light within us?

Reflection

If you have access to the Internet, check out the picture by Hanna Varghese at www.awrc4ct.org/artwork/hanna/canvas/3554005.htm. Spend some time with it, pondering what it says about the story. If you can't access the picture, take a few moments to imagine what kind of picture you would paint to capture the meeting of the two women.

Prayer

Teach me to listen to you, Lord. Let me hear your word. Help me to believe. Give me the legs to run and the arms to praise and good friends with whom to share the news. Let the joy of heaven come down to my earth!

✛

21 December

Magnificent hope

And Mary said, 'My soul magnifies the Lord, and my spirit rejoices in God my Saviour, for he has looked with favour on the lowliness of his servant. Surely, from now on all generations will call me blessed; for the Mighty One has done great things for me, and holy is his name. His mercy is for those who fear him from generation to generation. He has shown strength with his arm; he has scattered the proud in the thoughts of their hearts. He has brought down the powerful from their thrones, and lifted up the lowly; he has filled the hungry with good things, and sent the rich away empty. He has helped his servant Israel, in remembrance of his mercy, according to the promise he made to our ancestors, to Abraham and to his descendants forever.' And Mary remained with her for about three months and then returned to her home.

LUKE 1:46–56

Some of the stories that we love most are those in which the small, the vulnerable and the insignificant unexpectedly find themselves no longer at the bottom of the heap but actually winning and achieving. There is something in us that sighs with relief at a story that reassures us that those unjustly treated are finally vindicated and the perpetrators of that injustice have their comeuppance. The reason we long for this to happen is that too often it is not the humble who win but the arrogant; it is not the poor who succeed but the rich; it is not the weak who flourish but the strong. The longing for justice resides deep in the human heart.

The song that Mary sings, recorded in today's passage, springs from just such an instinct. Why are she and Elizabeth—and their unborn babies—leaping around with such delight and excitement? In part it is undoubtedly sheer delight at being with child. For Elizabeth there is the added wonder of such an event when she had thought her child-bearing days were long gone. For Mary there is the astonishment of knowing that she is carrying a very special child indeed. We might well expect Mary (and Elizabeth) to be singing at this point. The words that Luke has recorded for us are known as 'The Magnificat' (after the Latin translation of the opening words), and many Anglicans sing it regularly as part of their evening worship—in my experience, without the leaping, laughing delight of Mary and Elizabeth. While it is no surprise that Mary should sing, what is surprising is the content of her song. I would have expected her to sing a song about God's performing a miracle with this conception, of the fact that the long years of waiting for the Messiah are coming to an end and that people will be saved from their sins. But what actually excites her most is that at last justice is going to be done.

Mary is amazed and delighted that God should have chosen someone like her (v. 48). The fact that this delights her suggests that she, in common with most of her religious kinsfolk, was expecting the Messiah to come initially to the great, the mighty and the politically influential. Through Gabriel's visitation, however, Mary knows quite definitely that God's way of working is through this humble young girl from a run-down town on the margins of the world. God has not only noticed those on the margins—he has actually *chosen* them above the people at the centre of the world's powers. When Mary says, 'surely... all generations will call me blessed' (v. 48), she is not inviting centuries of admiration and devotion. We know that that is not in her character. What she is declaring here is that young and old, and generations to come, will notice that God chose to bless a young Nazarene girl, and therefore all people whom the world judges as insignificant and irrelevant are likely to be blessed by God, too. To the millions of other 'Marys' around the world, this is wonderful news.

Mary has clearly been reflecting on all this during her rushed journey over the hills to Elizabeth's home and has become increasingly aware of the consequences. Because God has chosen Mary for this most important of tasks, this means good news for the humble and the poor, and bad news for the proud, the powerful and the wealthy. God has started a process that will one day find complete fulfilment: the coming of God into the world is going to expose what is inside the minds of the proud—it will reveal the 'thoughts of their hearts' (v. 51), and there is no doubt that this is exactly what happened in those three years of ministry by her grown-up son Jesus. Whether it was the Pharisees, Pilate or Herod, those who were arrogant and who abused their power were confronted by Jesus. He was not afraid to call the fraudulent religious leaders 'whitewashed tombs, which on the outside look beautiful, but inside they are full of the bones of the dead and of all kinds of filth' (Matthew 23:27). On the outside the lives of these religious leaders looked fine and pure, but once you stripped away the whitewash, all you found was corruption. For the proud and powerful, Jesus and his kingdom were truly threatening, but for the poor and defenceless he brought healing, help and hope.

Twice in her song (Luke 1:50 and 54) Mary refers to the mercy of God. Mercy is about compassion, kindness and forgiveness. It is quite the opposite of what drives the arrogant, and what Mary is observing here is that the mercy of God, which goes right back to the days of Abraham, is with us forever. It is the controlling power of the universe and always will be. As you look around the world today, you may not feel that mercy is much in evidence. You may see many other kinds of power at work: militant extremists, making their point through acts of hideous violence; economists gambling on stock exchanges and selling currencies; whoever happens to be on the front cover of a celebrity magazine. But mercy? Well, that just seems like an idea that is all too easily pushed to the background. And yet, like Mary we can trust that God's justice and mercy will triumph in the end.

Mary stayed with her cousin for the final trimester of Elizabeth's pregnancy; no doubt she was a great help to Elizabeth in those final days. In the midst of all the chat about babies, there must also have been prayers and conversations expressing their hopes and longings. They would have watched the angry Roman soldiers march by, meting out petty punishments to the poor, and they would have witnessed local Pharisees piling spiritual burdens on those struggling to live well. But in their hearts they now knew of the sure existence of another world, a world that their sons were going to shape.

Reflection

Think about films you have seen and books you have read. Which ones best express the themes of the Magnificat? Explore what it is about them that moves you. Think of your longings for a more just and better world. Is there anything that the God of mercy is calling you to do today to help fulfil those longings?

Prayer

My soul is stirred to such joy in God,
For I have discovered that he is the kind of God who is concerned for one like me.
He has a special place for those who feel they have never been noticed and are always on the margins.
He truly is a God of mercy and will in time bring justice to this world, uprooting the arrogant and corrupt,
So that the humble will win
The hungry will be fed
And the poor will have all they need.
This mercy will always be around, and one day will be established fully and forever.

✣

Nativity

We have had the announcement of the births of John the Baptist and Jesus, and the celebrations surrounding these announcements. This week we move into the well-known stories of both these births, and if you have started reading this book at the beginning of December, this week you will be celebrating Christmas, and along with the stockings, the parcels, the turkey and the port, you will catch again the refrain of the old old story of the child born in a stable, born in the silent night—the Son of God, love's pure light.

I love the hymn 'Thorns in the Straw' by Graham Kendrick, which ponders what was going on in Mary's mind during these extraordinary days. In the words of this song, he imagines Mary's laying her child down to sleep and wondering if this life will always be a mixture of bitter and sweet. The song takes us on to the last days of her son's earthly life where she cradles not a newborn in her arms but finds herself at the foot of a cross, cradling the mortal remains of the son she brought into this world. The words that particularly touch me are as follows:

> *And did she see there*
> *In the straw by his head a thorn*
> *And did she smell myrrh*
> *In the air on that starry night*
> *And did she hear angels sing*
> *Not so far away*
> *Till at last the sun rose blood-red*
> *In the morning sky*[22]

The well-known events that we shall be reading about over the next couple of weeks are indeed bitter-sweet. We enter into the sheer wonder of new life, but we also hear anxious prophetic insights about a troubled road ahead. There is the colour of blood in the colours of the sunrise.

The good news is found in and through the bad news. These stories urge us to face honestly the bad news of a world where too many have preferred darkness to light, but they also demonstrate so clearly the power of hope that can truly transform the world around us.

✤

Breaking with tradition

Now the time came for Elizabeth to give birth, and she bore a son. Her neighbours and relatives heard that the Lord had shown his great mercy to her, and they rejoiced with her. On the eighth day they came to circumcise the child, and they were going to name him Zechariah after his father. But his mother said, 'No; he is to be called John.' They said to her, 'None of your relatives has this name.' Then they began motioning to his father to find out what name he wanted to give him. He asked for a writing tablet and wrote, 'His name is John.' And all of them were amazed. Immediately his mouth was opened and his tongue freed, and he began to speak, praising God. Fear came over all their neighbours, and all these things were talked about throughout the entire hill country of Judea. All who heard them pondered them and said, 'What then will this child become?' For, indeed, the hand of the Lord was with him.

LUKE 1:57–66

Today we return to the story of John the Baptist. Mary has left the home of Elizabeth and Zechariah and is back with her family, no doubt much strengthened from her three months with her cousin. As predicted, Elizabeth gives birth to a son. In the culture of that day, when the time of the birth was near, friends and local musicians would gather near the house. When the birth was announced, the musicians struck up and the celebrations began, and because Elizabeth had waited so long for a child, the celebrations must have been even more festive than normal.

Elizabeth and Zechariah were devout Jews and lived according to the law, which included the ceremony of circumcision for male children. This ceremony had to take place eight days after the birth;

it not only made a physical mark on the boy that he would carry all his life, but it was also a naming ceremony. Traditionally, the father pronounced the name of the son, but of course in Zechariah's case this was difficult because he had been struck dumb by the angel due to his unbelief (v. 20). The family present seem to have assumed that Zechariah's loss of speech meant he would not try to communicate a name, so they took it upon themselves to name the child Zechariah, after his father, as was the custom. Although it was acceptable to introduce another name, this was usually done only if there was some special significance in the new name.

So in today's passage the family are just about to name the child Zechariah, when Elizabeth protests, 'No, his name is to be John' (v. 60). The family are puzzled by this. They can't think of any relative who has been called John and they may not have been too keen on this name! They turn to Zechariah and make signs to him; the fact that they 'motion' to him rather than asking him directly suggests either that Zechariah had become deaf as well as speechless, or that his family are making the foolish assumption that because he can't talk, he can't hear either. It seems that since his encounter with the angel, Zechariah has taken something of a back seat in the story. You almost get the feeling here that they have to go and find him. But now energy starts to return to the old man. He indicates that he needs a writing tablet, and quite clearly and unequivocally puts, 'His name is John' (v. 63). We are told that the people are astonished by this and I wonder if it is more than the fact that he has chosen to use a non-family name. Maybe the way Zechariah phrases the message tells them that *he* is not giving the child this name, but someone else is. This is a child whose name is John, and he has been called that all his existence, because it is God, not a human, who has given him this name. And the name itself has significance: 'John' is the shorter form of 'Jehohanan', which means 'gift of God' and 'God is gracious'. It is indeed a prophetic name, for John will be a great gift to the world, with his task of preparing the people to meet the love of God made flesh in Jesus.

As the family group looks on and maybe begins to appreciate that there is something very special and God-blessed about this child, a remarkable thing happens: Zechariah, who has not been able to utter a word for the last nine months, can suddenly speak again. Not only does he speak but, as we shall see tomorrow, he starts to praise God with the most beautiful poetry. With Zechariah praising God perhaps as noisily as Elizabeth did when she met Mary, the child is duly circumcised and given the name John, and a sense of awe falls on the whole neighbourhood. They realize that this is not just a normal happy story of the birth of a much longed-for child; they are beginning to see that there is a truly miraculous aspect to these events and they all start speculating about what kind of a man this child will grow up to be. No doubt, even then, there were some wondering if he was the Messiah, a question that would be asked of him when he was an adult (3:15).

I love Zechariah's part in this story. I can't help feeling that the penalty of losing his speech for asking a simple question of the angel (Luke 1:20) seems rather harsh. Perhaps it was so that Zechariah wouldn't go spreading words of doubt. But, as ever, I think there is a pastoral side to this divine activity. By taking away Zechariah's speech, the angel is sending him into a world where he will spend most of his time listening. When neighbours come down and have a cup of wine at his home, all he can do is listen and nod and make signs and the odd note on a writing tablet. When they go for a stroll together in the evening light, it will be Elizabeth who is doing the talking, and Zechariah will have to listen. In the synagogue, he won't be able to join in the prayers and songs; he'll have to listen again. And I sense that little by little Zechariah begins to listen to life at a far deeper level. It is clear from his song, which we shall read tomorrow, that in his nine-month silence Zechariah has been spending much time dwelling on the meaning of the birth of his child. It is as if he has had a nine-month silent retreat during which he has discovered some wonderful truths about his son and about God's purposes for this world.

In the busy, noisy and talkative world where we live there is an increasing yearning for silence and stillness, and more and more people want to go to convents and monasteries where they don't have to talk, but where they can simply worship, think and listen to God for a few days. Zechariah had nine months, and most of us only get a few days, but in my experience, even 24 hours of silence means that I start to hear things I never notice in the days when I talk too much and listen too little. In this way, the silent Zechariah has much to say to us all.

Reflection

If you haven't done it before, why not try to get away for at least 24 hours of silence? How do you feel about this? What do you think you might begin to hear? If you do go away from time to time on silent retreats, remind yourself today about what you heard on those retreats. Were there some important themes you need to remember? Are there some words from God that you need to bring to mind?

Prayer

Lord, when I talk too much, shut me up! Give me some good spaces of silence, where I can go deeper, listen longer and thereby live better.

❖

23 December

A light for those in darkness

Then his father Zechariah was filled with the Holy Spirit and spoke this prophecy: 'Blessed be the Lord God of Israel, for he has looked favourably on his people and redeemed them. He has raised up a mighty saviour for us in the house of his servant David, as he spoke through the mouth of his holy prophets from of old, that we would be saved from our enemies and from the hand of all who hate us. Thus he has shown the mercy promised to our ancestors, and has remembered his holy covenant, the oath that he swore to our ancestor Abraham, to grant us that we, being rescued from the hands of our enemies, might serve him without fear, in holiness and righteousness before him all our days. And you, child, will be called the prophet of the Most High; for you will go before the Lord to prepare his ways, to give knowledge of salvation to his people by the forgiveness of their sins. By the tender mercy of our God, the dawn from on high will break upon us, to give light to those who sit in darkness and in the shadow of death, to guide our feet into the way of peace.'

LUKE 1:67–79

The lips that were sealed for nine months are now opened. I don't know if Zechariah was a natural poet, but I suspect not. I suspect that those months of enforced silence took him to a new quality of life. Without a fundamental means of communication, he had to learn to use other gifts and instincts that were latent within him, and in using those he made some dramatic discoveries.

Zechariah lost his speech only temporarily, but it was long enough for him to delve into his priestly soul and discover a rich mixture of hopes, longings, insights and prophecies that he delivers in his poem. It starts off with a declaration of delight: God has decided to redeem his people and the many promises delivered by prophets over many centuries are now about to be fulfilled.

It's quite likely that in his months of silence, Zechariah went back over the old prophets and books of the law and read them in a new light. They were no longer just interesting old manuscripts; they were no longer remarkable religious writings that made sense only to theologians and important people; they had now come alive. For example, he may have gone back to the writings of the prophet Jeremiah who predicted that one day God would raise up a king who would reign wisely and do what is just and right in the land (Jeremiah 23:5). People of faith at the time of Zechariah would often read such passages. They were oppressed by foreign occupation and longed for freedom, but they must have often felt that the oppression they experienced was very long-term, and any deliverance was a long way off. As Zechariah holds those ancient promises alongside his extraordinary experience of the angel in the temple and the gift of his son, he begins to hear a new message: God is acting here and now! All that was written by the prophets and all that was promised to the ancestors is now about to be fulfilled in the midst of ordinary everyday life.

As Zechariah celebrates that this greatest of moments has arrived, he himself becomes a prophet and speaks directly to his young son John. This little boy is to be the 'prophet of the Most High' (Luke 1:76). Mary was told by Gabriel that her son would be the 'Son of the Most High' (v. 32). This term 'Most High' was a term often used of God. Devout Jews do not use the name of God ('Yahweh') because it is deemed too holy to utter, so they use other names that describe him. The 'Most High' term is one that emphasizes the greatness of his power and majesty. Zechariah prophesies to his son that he will have a role of preparing the way for the Most High. In other words, this God who is Most High, who dwells in heaven, is to visit lowly earth, and Zechariah's child is the one who is to get things ready for this extraordinary visitation. The message is now starting to get through to Zechariah and others involved in this story that God really is visiting earth, and the way he is choosing to do so is not through the high and mighty, but through the humble and lowly.

Twice in Zechariah's song he refers to mercy (vv. 72 and 78); Mary also uses this word twice in her song. When we use this word nowadays, it tends to be in the sense of someone being let off a punishment. Many a time in old films we see some poor victim facing death, crying out, 'Please, have mercy.' A rather stern figure of authority then begrudgingly agrees to be lenient and spare them. So when 'mercy' is used of God, we can end up thinking of a rather fierce, authoritarian God being persuaded not to punish us. But although there is a sense of pardon in the Hebrew and Greek words for mercy, the meaning is more to do with compassion and kindness. The emphasis, therefore, is not on God choosing not to punish, but rather on God drawing near to us in our suffering and showing kindness. The final beautiful verses of Zechariah's song are about the compassion of God being like the sun rising on a wounded land, and making its way into the darkest valleys of sorrow and suffering, including that valley of the shadow of death. The result of this light shining is the great gift of peace.

This shows yet again how Zechariah has been on a spiritual journey in the months of Elizabeth's pregnancy. He has moved from the shock of the angelic visitation, when he was gripped with fear (v. 12) and doubted the angel's word (v. 18), to become a man filled with excitement at the news of a God who is coming into this world in the most tender of ways, expressing his compassion to those who find themselves in valleys of many kinds.

Like Zechariah, we can develop hitherto underused parts of ourselves in such a way that we make new discoveries about this world and about God. We can very easily settle into our well-established views and opinions about faith and life, but sometimes it is good to step to one side of our usual pathways and give ourselves the opportunity to discover fresh insights. We may not be struck dumb like Zechariah, but we can try to stop talking so much and delivering our opinions, and to give more time to listening to others and to God and seeing what we discover as a result. We may reflect on how we use our senses and ask ourselves which of them are underused in our lives. There may be ways in which we can learn to see more, hear more, touch more, feel more, and taste more.

Reflection

Have any of your senses been underused? Are you able to put aside your tried and tested ways of exploring this world and the God who made it, and try using other, less familiar ways?

Prayer

There is so much I don't know, Lord, and so much I don't see, don't hear and don't feel. Visit me today and bring to life those parts of me that have lain dormant for too long that I may discover you and this world in new ways.

✢

Census and sensibility

In those days a decree went out from Emperor Augustus that all the world should be registered. This was the first registration and was taken while Quirinius was governor of Syria. All went to their own towns to be registered. Joseph also went from the town of Nazareth in Galilee to Judea, to the city of David called Bethlehem, because he was descended from the house and family of David. He went to be registered with Mary, to whom he was engaged and who was expecting a child. While they were there, the time came for her to deliver her child. And she gave birth to her firstborn son and wrapped him in bands of cloth, and laid him in a manger, because there was no place for them in the inn.

LUKE 2:1–7

We now arrive at the birth of Jesus, and Luke takes us back to the world of political power and the defenceless poor. For most people who lived in Judaea, Rome might as well have been another planet. It was geographically a long way away, and culturally its life, values, politics and religion were totally different from that of Palestine. Despite its difference and its distance, its presence was most definitely felt, and from time to time decrees would come from Rome that caused huge upheaval.

In the Roman Empire censuses were taken with the aim of assessing taxation and of finding out who was suitable for military service. In other words, the aims were generally to do with increasing money and power. The Jews were exempt from military service, so in Palestine the census was largely about money, and that would mostly be seen as wealthy Rome taking more money off those they had conquered. Luke tells us that everyone went to 'their own towns' (v. 3), explaining that in Joseph's case this meant a trip to Bethlehem, which was about 80 miles from Nazareth, at least a three-day trek. So there were thousands like Joseph who were forced into long journeys to give their details to Roman officials with the most likely net result that they would have to pay higher taxes to those occupying their land. There must have been intense resentment about this, and it is not surprising that regular insurrections took place against the Romans precisely in response to this kind of decree.

For Joseph and Mary this must have been about the worst piece of news they could have received. Mary was clearly very close to giving birth and she must have known there was a real likelihood that she might bear her child at some point on the journey. Perhaps they were both safeguarded by a sense of peace. After all, this had all begun in a supernatural way and no doubt God was directing affairs. They would have seen the significance of Bethlehem, the city of David, being the birthplace of the Messiah. At the same time they must have wished that God had organized it in a more comfortable and convenient way. Did they have secret doubts? When there was no room for them in the inn, did they worry that they had not heard God clearly? Was Joseph berating himself with thoughts like, 'I knew we should have left sooner'?

The story is so well known that it is hardly worth describing, but perhaps if we put it into a modern setting we might get closer to its original impact. Imagine that Mary and Joseph were living in Inverness and they discovered they had to register in Salisbury. They borrow an old Mini from a friend, and it takes them three days to potter down to Salisbury, with Mary lying in the back seat trying every possible contortion to get comfortable. When they reach Salisbury all the Bed and Breakfasts are full, although they find one where they are told that there is some room in the garage. It's raining and cold and any shelter is welcome. So, parking their Mini on the road, they make their way into the garage and Joseph finds a handy cardboard box and he is grateful to find a pile of old sheets and blankets. The time for the birth is upon them, and Mary lies on a blanket that protects her a little from the cold and oil-stained garage floor. A single 40-watt bulb gives just enough light for Joseph to do the work of a midwife. Together these two young people in most unpromising circumstances usher a little boy into the world. Joseph cuts the cord and quickly wraps the baby in the old sheets and hands him to his exhausted mother. The joy of holding her firstborn now overshadows the pain of childbirth and the discomfort of the gloomy garage. They feel not only delighted with the safe arrival of this new little life, but they give thanks that they have managed to deliver him safely despite the most adverse circumstances.

I can hear lots of people saying, 'Ah well, in those days they were used to such difficulties...' and so on, but despite their familiarity with discomforts of many kinds, I can't help feeling admiration for this young couple. What was really going through their minds during this experience? We know the story ended happily, but when they were in the middle of it, they must have wondered if God couldn't have arranged for a slightly easier and safer route for his son's arrival in this world. After all, it was a big enough leap as it was for God to come to earth as a baby, but to do so in such precarious circumstances seemed one peril too many. Why take such risks? Was it really necessary for Mary to travel during the last stage of her pregnancy? Was God so remote that he didn't understand what it was like to carry a child? Was he testing Mary and Joseph just to make sure they were strong enough? If so, what would he have done had they failed the test at this stage? Did Mary and Joseph ask these questions about God? Maybe they were so full of faith and confidence in God that they did not, and it is only those of lesser faith, like me, who think about such issues.

Perhaps there was something else going on. Perhaps God has such a special love for those who are struggling, those whose lives are controlled by more powerful people, those who live in places of danger, those who feel immensely vulnerable in this world, that he chose to do it *their* way. To do it *their* way would surely demonstrate that he really had within his divine nature a sensibility to human struggle and suffering and was on the side of the outsider, the vulnerable, and the powerless. I think this was the message that Mary had heard originally. She knew he was the God who brought down the powerful from their thrones and lifted up the lowly (1:52). Here he was now identifying with the lowly as a way of empowering them, and his very presence as a vulnerable child did indeed have an immediate effect, for it was enough to threaten the powerful Herod who was terrified that this baby would knock him off his throne (see Matthew 2:1–18).

It is particularly sad that Christianity, once it started to become the state religion in different countries of the world, became associated with political power and wealth, and there have been too many shameful stories in our Church history due to our straying away from the values so clearly demonstrated in this story. Despite all this, there have always been little Christian protest movements that have pushed past that human temptation to connect religion and worldly power, and have reminded us of the God who really is on the side of the weak. And that is a real point of hope for those times in our lives when we feel that much is loaded against us.

Reflection

How do you imagine this story happening? What do you think was going on in Mary and Joseph's minds? What would you have said to them to encourage them on that journey to Bethlehem? How does the message of Jesus born as an outcast help you?

Prayer

Father in heaven, you took such a risk to show us how much you want to draw near to us in our places of brokenness. When I am in such a place, help me to discover your presence that we may journey on together.

✣

25 December

Hillside revelations

In that region there were shepherds living in the fields, keeping watch over their flock by night. Then an angel of the Lord stood before them, and the glory of the Lord shone around them, and they were terrified. But the angel said to them, 'Do not be afraid; for see—I am bringing you good news of great joy for all the people: to you is born this day in the city of David a Saviour, who is the Messiah, the Lord. This will be a sign for you: you will find a child wrapped in bands of cloth and lying in a manger.' And suddenly there was with the angel a multitude of the heavenly host, praising God and saying, 'Glory to God in the highest heaven, and on earth peace among those whom he favours!' When the angels had left them and gone into heaven, the shepherds said to one another, 'Let us go now to Bethlehem and see this thing that has taken place, which the Lord has made known to us.' So they went with haste and found Mary and Joseph, and the child lying in the manger. When they saw this, they made known what had been told them about this child; and all who heard it were amazed at what the shepherds told them. But Mary treasured all these words and pondered them in her heart. The shepherds returned, glorifying and praising God for all they had heard and seen, as it had been told them.
LUKE 2:8–20

Luke now takes us away from the hubbub of Bethlehem for a moment to the relative quiet of the surrounding hillside, where we find ourselves among a group of shepherds. Although shepherds were an integral part of the culture of the day, they were viewed by those in religious authority as outcasts. The reason for this was purely practical: they couldn't engage in the various washing and cleaning rituals that were required by the law, and the constant demands of their flocks meant that they missed important religious observances. So in the eyes of the strict religious rulers such as the Pharisees, these men were unclean. However, they may well have been caring for sheep which would have been used for the ritual sacrifices in the temple in Jerusalem, because the sheep used in these sacrifices were pastured near Bethlehem. If this was the case then the shepherds' occupation could be seen as a curious mixture of sacred and profane.

How much of this was relevant to these particular shepherds we don't know. They were most likely just a group of normal blokes who were grateful for a relatively steady job despite long hours and hard work. Part of that work included night duty, where they would sleep alongside their flocks, always alert to the presence of any predators. Presumably this particular night started like any other—chatter around the camp fire, putting of the world to rights. Suddenly they are in the presence of an angel. Luke's readers are now starting to get used to the angel of the Lord popping up in unexpected places, so for us it is less surprising. For these shepherds, however, it was clearly a massive shock! This time, the angel–human encounter is not a one-to-one meeting in a private place as it was with Mary, nor is it in the sacred space of the temple as it was with Zechariah. Here the angel appears in the open for everyone to see, and not only that, but the glory of the Lord is shining all around.

In the Old Testament there are several references to the glory of God. In Exodus 16:7 and 10, for example, there are references to the glory of God that is leading the Israelites through the wilderness. The New Testament also has references to this kind of glory, most notably in the episode of the transfiguration of Jesus (Luke 9:28–36), that extraordinary story of Jesus on the mountainside being transformed by a cloud of glory. It's quite hard to define what this glory is, but it seems to appear when God's presence is so strong that it takes on an almost tangible, visible aspect. Throughout the history of the Church, up until the present day, there are stories of people witnessing this kind of glory, and to read about or hear about such incidents can be very moving. People describe it in various ways—awesome, frightening, reassuring, loving, although they would often say they don't have words to describe it. Whatever it is, the shepherds clearly knew that it wasn't a usual occurrence on a Bethlehem hillside in the evening, and for them it was initially terrifying.

The angel has a simple message to give: 'I am bringing you good news of great joy' (2:10). I would love to have paused the conversation at that point and asked each shepherd what would be the best news they could have received. Maybe one would say it would be winning whatever the equivalent of the lottery was in those days; another might say it would be hearing that the Romans were moving out; for another, it might have been hearing that his very sick wife had been miraculously cured. Who knows what they might have said, but all of us harbour hopes and longings, and when someone comes along with good news, our hopes will always rise.

Well, the angel gives them the good news and it is this: the Messiah has come, and not only has he come, but he has come to Bethlehem, and he has come as a newborn baby lying in a cattle-feeding trough. The shepherds are not given a chance to respond at this point because heaven just can't contain its excitement anymore. Suddenly a huge number of angels, hitherto hidden from sight, appear and fill the air with their song, which is all about glory and peace. Luke doesn't say whether they sing or say this message, but I imagine they would be singing. I've met a few people who say they have heard angels singing, and they tell me that the sound is too beautiful to describe. So here are the shepherds, who only moments ago were idly chatting to one another around the fire, and they are now witnessing the most majestic celestial concert and hearing the news that the Messiah has come.

I get the impression that just as the party seems to be reaching a crescendo, it suddenly stops and the angels vanish as quickly as they appeared. I can see the shepherds standing by their fire, blinking foolishly at each other until one of them says, 'Come on, let's go and see this baby.' I wonder if the angel gave them more specific instructions, as there must have been no end of stables in Bethlehem, and not a few newborn babies in a town filled with visitors coming for the census. Well, whether they were given instructions, or whether a residual influence of the glory of God left a kind of satnav instinct in them, one way or another they find themselves in that back street stable, staring at a tiny baby in the arms of a young mother.

What has always touched me about this story is the contrast between the highly dramatic and the very ordinary. The shepherds witness an amazing heavenly concert, but what gets them really excited is not the display of angels on the hillside, but the very domestic scene of the mother and baby. It is, of course, the message of the angels that makes that scene so special, and this in itself is significant. Few of us are likely to see the heavenly host and come across the angel of the Lord giving us a personal message. But we can all have moments of being unusually aware of what some call the 'numinous'—a sense of the presence of God. It may come as we are going about our normal lives, or we may find we encounter it when we are in a particularly holy place or at a very important moment in life. It's not something we can manufacture; we can't create the experience. It is a gift and we can be either open or closed to receiving it. Some encounters, like the experience of the shepherds, are so dramatic that you would have to be incredibly unaware to miss it. But other encounters are much more subtle. They are precious moments when it feels as if God has just slipped into the room and is beside us, when we become more open to his presence, when the veil between this world and heaven seems far thinner than normal. When these moments happen it is worth stopping whatever we are doing and being as receptive as we can. There may be a message for us or a sign that we must follow. The hillside experience gave the shepherds new eyes. After that experience they could go into the streets of Bethlehem and find a perfectly normal domestic scene but see it with the eyes of heaven. They found the Messiah in the stable—they found God in the ordinary. This is the great gift of the heavenly encounter—it enables us to discover the presence of God in the most mundane of places.

Reflection

Have you ever had moments when you have sensed the presence of God in a very special way? You may have valued it at the time, or you may have dismissed it, even been frightened of it. What do you think God was trying to say to you? Think about what you will be doing in the next few days— how can you live in such a way as to be more open to seeing the signs of God in the events of daily life?

Prayer

Open my heart, Lord, so that I may discover your presence and hear your word to me, whether in hillside revelations or in the everyday streets of my world.

✛

26 December

Dazzled at evensong

After eight days had passed, it was time to circumcise the child; and he was called Jesus, the name given by the angel before he was conceived in the womb. When the time came for their purification according to the law of Moses, they brought him up to Jerusalem to present him to the Lord (as it is written in the law of the Lord, 'Every firstborn male shall be designated as holy to the Lord'), and they offered a sacrifice according to what is stated in the law of the Lord, 'a pair of turtle-doves or two young pigeons.' Now there was a man in Jerusalem whose name was Simeon; this man was righteous and devout, looking forward to the consolation of Israel, and the Holy Spirit rested on him. It had been revealed to him by the Holy Spirit that he would not see death before he had seen the Lord's Messiah. Guided by the Spirit, Simeon came into the temple; and when the parents brought in the child Jesus, to do for him what was customary under the law, Simeon took him in his arms and praised God, saying, 'Master, now you are dismissing your servant in peace, according to your word; for my eyes have seen your salvation, which you have prepared in the presence of all peoples, a light for revelation to the Gentiles and for glory to your people Israel.' And the child's father and mother were amazed at what was being said about him. Then Simeon blessed them and said to his mother Mary, 'This child is destined for the falling and the rising of many in Israel, and to be a sign that will be opposed so that the inner thoughts of many will be revealed—and a sword will pierce your own soul too.'

LUKE 2:21–35

Mary and Joseph were faithful Jews, therefore they took their son to the temple in Jerusalem to undertake the three ceremonies that were required by the law. Firstly, there was the circumcision that happened to every boy eight days after his birth. The child was also given his name at this occasion. Secondly, there was 'the redemption of the firstborn'. This was to fulfil the law described in Exodus 13:2, which declared that every firstborn was sacred to God and belonged to him, in recognition that all life came from God. Accordingly, the parents had to 'buy back' their child from God and a token sum of money was paid. Thirdly, there was the ritual called 'the purification after childbirth'. When a woman had given birth to a child she was considered 'unclean' for a period of time. At the end of this time, she had to bring a sacrifice to the temple. Usually she would offer a lamb, but those who were very poor could bring 'the offering of the poor', which was two pigeons (Leviticus 12:1–7). The fact that Mary and Joseph brought two pigeons is one of the clues that tells us that they were indeed poor.

We may find these ancient rituals uncomfortable reading, but we should remember that they were all about acknowledging that the child was a gift from God. So here once again we have an everyday scene, one that would have happened all the time, and again, this scene is transformed because of the unique child who is the focus of our story. For most people in the temple that day, there was nothing extraordinary about this little family coming to do their religious duty: just a mother and father grateful for the gift of a precious life. But there was someone in the temple who was on the lookout for something special and his name was Simeon. The very name tells us something about the man, for the Hebrew root of the name means 'listener', and he was indeed someone who spent a great deal of time listening. Some say that he was likely to be one of the 'Quiet of the Land'. This was a group of contemplative people who spent much time in prayer and devotion and who nursed in their hearts a longing to see the Messiah come to earth. Whereas the zealots expected the Messiah to come with armies and military victories, purging the land from the stain of the pagan Romans, the Quiet of the Land expected God to come peacefully. They knew they had to be always on the lookout, because they believed he would not come with great signs from heaven, but more discreetly, to be recognized by those who had eyes to see.

Simeon was certainly this quiet, prayerful contemplative type, and it sounds as if he had spent much of his life coming to the temple, listening, watching and longing for the signs of God. At one moment in his life, he heard a personal word from God, that he would see the Messiah before he died (Luke 1:26). I imagine Simeon as an old man, clinging tight to that promise and going day by day to the temple to find a quiet place to watch and pray. As he got older, did be begin to have his doubts? Did he begin to wonder whether he had heard correctly? As his eyes started to fail, did he occasionally wonder whether he really would see the Messiah? Did he start to reinterpret the message he had received? Maybe it meant something more spiritual—that he wouldn't literally see the Messiah but simply get a 'sense' of the presence of the Messiah? I am sure he must have had his moments of doubt, but something about this story suggests that Simeon had a deep conviction about seeing the Messiah, and he was determined to stay around until he had seen him.

And so it is that one day his faith and patience are rewarded. The Messiah has entered the world and comes to the place of worship. He has not come with mighty fanfares, cosmic signs and angelic bands, sweeping Roman battalions to one side in his wake. No, he comes in the arms of a young mother from Galilee, who is one of the poorest of the land. Simeon watches the family take the baby through the initiation rituals and then goes up to them and takes the newborn child in his aged arms, looks up to heaven and praises God in words that have been recounted and used in worship for 2000 years.

The song of praise in verses 29 to 32 is known in many churches as the 'Nunc Dimittis' (after the first two words of the Latin version) and for centuries it has been said or sung in evening services. It is a song sung by an old man in the evening of his life, and in this song he is not lamenting the coming darkness of death and night but is celebrating the dazzling power of light and life. His eyes have now seen that which he has been longing for—a light that will light up both Gentiles and Jews, indeed the whole world. This Messiah is not just for the established religion of that region, or for a privileged few. He will be a bright light for all to see. As Simeon exults in this revelation, he then looks at the young mother and father who are clearly astonished by what is happening (v. 33), and you sense his voice dropping and taking a serious tone as he warns that there will be those who oppose this child and this opposition will be for Mary as a sword piercing her heart (v. 35). Who knows what was going through Mary's mind as she is drawn into the wonder and delight of Simeon's song of praise, but surely also into some anxiety about these sombre warnings?

One thing I notice about this story is Luke's interest in the activity of the Holy Spirit in Simeon's life. In verses 25 to 27 the Holy Spirit is upon Simeon, reveals truths to him and guides him to this little family. Simeon's quiet life of prayer had obviously allowed him to develop an extraordinary sensitivity to God's Holy Spirit. He could feel his movements like the slight breath of wind on a calm day. As a result he was truly prophetic—he could 'see' things that others could not and he was able to carry a very important message to a young family.

Not long ago, on a visit to Darjeeling in North India, my wife and I and the two friends with whom we were travelling were invited to a meal in the home of an elderly couple called Mr and Mrs Kumar. At that time of year Darjeeling was very cold and damp, being quite high up in the Himalayas, and it was hard to find anywhere to get warm. However, when we arrived at this home, there was a warm fire and delicious hot food. We were made to feel so welcome, not only by the couple, but also their family that had been extended over the years as young people became effectively adopted into this family. One of the 'sons' was a young man called Raul who had recently become a Christian. He told us his story of how he had come from a Muslim background. He found himself suffering greatly from depression and could find no freedom from it. From time to time he met Mr Kumar and could not help noticing that he was full of life. Raul was puzzled—here he was, a young man with his whole life before him but burdened by a dark depression; Mr Kumar had most of his life behind him, yet was so full of life. Eventually he asked Mr Kumar to tell him about the life he had, and Mr Kumar told Raul all about Jesus who gives his Holy Spirit to everyone who asks. Raul asked the old man to pray for him, which he did, asking Jesus to give him the streams of living water promised by Jesus in John 7:38. Raul told us of how he felt the Holy Spirit fill his soul, dispersing the darkness and filling him with wonderful light. He has never experienced depression since and now spends a lot of his time telling others about what God has done for him.

I thought how Mr Kumar was a kind of Simeon figure: a man towards the end of his life, yet full of the Spirit and ready and willing to share that Spirit with others. In the West we too often push the elderly to one side, presuming that they have done their work, and that energy and drive rests with the young. What Simeon and old Mr Kumar show us is that some old people have finally reached the stage where the Holy Spirit moves wonderfully and freely within them, and in this age of spiritual drought, we need them more than ever.

Reflection

Simeon was aware of his longings. What are yours? How open to the Spirit are you? What do you think you need to help you become more open to God's Spirit?

Prayer

Lord, I, too, have my longings and my dreams. May the Holy Spirit rest on me, that I may truly see, and may your Spirit move me to those places and people where I can share your rivers of living water.

·‡·

27 December

When I'm 84

There was also a prophet, Anna the daughter of Phanuel, of the tribe of Asher. She was of a great age, having lived with her husband seven years after her marriage, then as a widow to the age of eighty-four. She never left the temple but worshipped there with fasting and prayer night and day. At that moment she came, and began to praise God and to speak about the child to all who were looking for the redemption of Jerusalem. When they had finished everything required by the law of the Lord, they returned to Galilee, to their own town of Nazareth. The child grew and became strong, filled with wisdom; and the favour of God was upon him.

LUKE 2:36–38

A little while ago we reached a rather unsettling landmark: Paul McCartney became 64. There is nothing particularly remarkable in someone's becoming 64, but in Paul's case it was significant, because as a young man he had written and sung his well-known song 'When I'm 64' on *Sergeant Pepper's Lonely Hearts Club Band*, which came out in 1967. I was a teenager at the time and remember the release of the album very clearly. It was virtually mandatory to buy all the Beatles albums as they came out, but the problem for me was that at the time I was at a boarding school where we were not allowed record players. However, an enterprising friend of mine smuggled a very small battery-operated player into school, and we cycled off to some fields at a safe distance from the school and lay in the grass listening to the tracks over and over again.

At that time, as a teenager in the 1960s, the age of 64 seemed impossibly old, an age that people like us would never reach, and we would view such far-off days with light-hearted humour. In his song

Paul took us into the world of a retired couple who would do gardening, enjoy grandchildren and scrimp and save to have holidays on the Isle of Wight. Much of the song described a state of contentment in retirement, but there were also some expressions of anxiety such as 'yours sincerely, wasting away', and of course that questioning chorus, 'Will you still need me, will you still feed me, when I'm sixty-four?' Of course the irony was that when Paul McCartney did reach 64 he had lost his beloved wife, Linda, and his present marriage was in disarray, and the song seemed therefore very poignant.

In our Bible story today, our central character is 20 years on from 64 and, in a time when people died younger, that was a great age indeed. But she had been a teenager once, and she would have imagined her future. We are told by Luke that she was married but that her husband died after only seven years. It was the custom at the time to marry young, and therefore she would almost certainly have been a widow in her early twenties. As a young married woman she would have had her dreams of a fulfilled life with children and a happy retirement with grandchildren, still needing her husband, still feeding him at 64 and beyond. But these dreams were not to be. They were harshly cut short as her husband died, leaving her alone and vulnerable.

It is interesting that Luke tells us this bit of domestic information about Anna to give us a context for her ministry. I suspect the natural instinct of most of us today would be to feel sorry for this woman who had known widowhood for so much of her life. At the time, however, some would have assumed that such a tragedy must be a judgment from God, that she must have done something seriously wrong to offend God to provoke him to mete out such harsh punishment. Others might not have taken such an unsympathetic view, but they may have been rather patronizing, assuming that she could not have had a particularly satisfying life after such a tragedy. Sadly, there would have been some who would not have taken anything she said seriously, simply because she was a woman.

None of this stopped Anna from living a highly effective life. She must have suffered a bitter loss when her husband died at such a young age, but rather than writing her life off as of little use, she realized a new calling. She gave her tragedy to God and listened to him for direction. At first, she may have hoped that he would lead her to another husband, but clearly God had other plans for her life. He was calling her to a ministry of prayer and listening, and this was a calling she obeyed for the rest of her life. I expect there were those who looked at the young Anna and said, 'Such a shame,' as they saw her go day by day to the temple for fasting and prayer. There would have been others who would have doubted the effectiveness of her prayers, and no doubt some men who questioned whether God listened to a woman's prayers anyway. I am sure there were others who were deeply impressed by her and thanked God for her steadfastness and faith. There would be a similar range of response today to a young woman who felt called to join a convent. Recently I received a newsletter from a Roman Catholic community that I often visit, and I noticed a picture of one of the young members of the community in a bridal dress. The photo was celebrating her 'Bridal Day' when she made a life commitment to be 'single for the Lord'. Some would find this very hard to understand or accept, but I am sure that for this young woman the day was as happy as if she was being married to a man. She would understand Anna well.

Whatever the human responses, Anna persevered in her life of faith and devotion, and it is clear that, as with Simeon, she also nursed a longing and a hope to see the Messiah. The moment she saw him she ran over to him and prophesied to all who were nearby that this little baby would be the means through which God would rescue his people. Something in her spirit detected that this was no ordinary child. As with Simeon, her years of praying, yearning and listening meant that she could see in ways few others could, and in this little child she recognized the Messiah.

For Mary and Joseph this must have been extremely reassuring. Here they were as young parents entrusted with an extraordinary life, and here in the holy place of the temple, two gentle, elderly spiritual listeners had come and given their blessing. Mary and Joseph must have had their moments of wondering whether they were looking after Jesus correctly, but these kinds of prophetic signs would have been very affirming. It was as if God was saying to them, 'Well done. You are doing right. You are caring for my son well.'

This story brings to an end Luke's account of Jesus' arrival in the world as the baby in Bethlehem. He was heralded by angels, delighted in by shepherds, acknowledged as the Messiah by two aged prophets, and now Mary and Joseph return to Galilee, to their home town of Nazareth. Although Jesus apparently had wisdom well beyond his years (v. 40), nonetheless there was probably not a lot that distinguished the family from others in the neighbourhood. In that somewhat forgotten place, the life of the Messiah grew, and seeds of his remarkable ministry were gestating.

The stories of Simeon and Anna, and the years of Jesus' growing up in relative anonymity tell us something about God's view of time. Simeon spent years longing and looking out for the Messiah; Anna spent the long decades of her widowhood fasting and praying for people to be set free; Jesus passed quiet years in Nazareth, preparing for his ministry. Today, if something isn't fixed instantly, we get irritated. We need everything now and order things for next-day delivery. The thought of spending so much time waiting and preparing might seem like a waste. These stories tell us that there is real value in giving time to watching, listening and putting down roots.

Here in the Western world, we too often think of life as a long series of tasks—we go through each day ticking off our achievements and hope we'll make it to an old age when we can, like the couple in Paul McCartney's song, relax with gardening and grandchildren. Maybe it's not quite like that. Maybe it's not about ticking off achievements but rather about accumulating wisdom, growing in insight, listening to the longings of God for his world and developing skills to perceive signs of his activity and growing in courage to speak prophetically to those who have not yet acquired the eyes to see. In that way, 'when I get older, losing my hair many years from now' I will not be worried about 'wasting away', but quite the reverse. They will be years of cultivation rather than wasting, when I can look and see something of the fruit of my years of praying and yearning. Simeon and Anna stand for us as giants of hope for any who fear growing older, and they challenge a number of today's silly idolatries that will not respect the need for time and space.

Reflection

Think of someone you know who is elderly. What is it you appreciate in them? Is there anything about how they live that you admire? Is there anything about the way they live that you would want to avoid? If you are elderly, how do you feel about the ministries of Simeon and Anna?

Prayer

Lord, I thank you for this moment in time. Help me to pause, to draw breath and to take in all that you want to give me now. Let the way I live today make me wiser for tomorrow.

28 December

Losing Jesus

Now every year his parents went to Jerusalem for the festival of the Passover. And when he was twelve years old, they went up as usual for the festival. When the festival was ended and they started to return, the boy Jesus stayed behind in Jerusalem, but his parents did not know it. Assuming that he was in the group of travellers, they went a day's journey. Then they started to look for him among their relatives and friends. When they did not find him, they returned to Jerusalem to search for him. After three days they found him in the temple, sitting among the teachers, listening to them and asking them questions. And all who heard him were amazed at his understanding and his answers. When his parents saw him they were astonished; and his mother said to him, 'Child, why have you treated us like this? Look, your father and I have been searching for you in great anxiety.' He said to them, 'Why were you searching for me? Did you not know that I must be in my Father's house?' But they did not understand what he said to them. Then he went down with them and came to Nazareth, and was obedient to them. His mother treasured all these things in her heart.
LUKE 2:41–51

This is the one story of Jesus' childhood that we have and we find him at twelve years of age. Although today we consider twelve-year-olds still to be children, in the Jewish culture of the first century a Jewish boy became a man when he was twelve, which meant that he had to take on the obligations of the law. One of these obligations was to go to Jerusalem for the major festivals, and every man who lived within 15 miles of the great city had to attend the Passover. Although Jesus had been taken to Jerusalem as a baby, it is quite probable that this visit when he was twelve was the first time he was aware of the city and the temple, and it must have been a momentous occasion for him. How much did this boy know of who he was and what his mission in life was to be? There have been many books speculating on just how much self-knowledge Jesus had at different stages of his life, but certainly by this stage he had gained some considerable awareness and some sense of independence from his parents, for he stayed in the temple after his parents had left.

We often view this story from Mary and Joseph's point of view. Any of us who are parents can imagine how appalled we would feel at discovering that our child was not with us and that we had actually left him in a huge and busy city. It is understandable how this might have happened. People would have gone to the city for the festival in family groups and Mary and Joseph would each have assumed that the other or a member of the family was caring for Jesus. We get the impression that until that point Jesus was well behaved, and looking after him had probably been pretty easy. But when they discovered he was missing, they must have been frantic. Not only would they have had the normal horror of any parent at losing their child, but they must have also been wondering what God was thinking. He had entrusted his only son to them to care for him in a world they knew would be hostile. Those three days of searching through Jerusalem must have been quite dreadful for them, and they may well have had moments of fearing the worst. They had known the plans Herod had had to destroy him when he was little. Could there now be a successful attack upon him? As it turned out they need not have been so worried, because they eventually found him safe and sound in the temple precincts.

From Jesus' point of view the episode looks quite different. He has been taken to the holy city and there he is treated as a man and is permitted to take part in the various rituals associated with the festival that commemorated the act of liberation when God led his people out of slavery and through the Red Sea to begin their journey to the Promised Land. Even at this stage, Jesus must have had some awareness of his role in another act of deliverance that would one day take place in this city. This was a highly important time for him, when he could rub shoulders with theologians and pastors and listen to what they taught, and ask those questions his local rabbi at home couldn't answer. It also gave him a chance to share his thoughts and begin his work of helping people to understand more about God. He must have been in the temple precincts from dawn to dusk, engaged in conversation, all the time gaining more insight into the work that was being entrusted to him. We never know where he stayed at night, but no doubt some kind family took him in.

When Mary and Joseph finally catch up with him they do what any normal parents do on such occasions: they express their pent-up anxiety in anger. Just as we might say, 'Why didn't you stay where I told you to? I've told you before not to wander off, and never to talk to strangers,' so Mary says to Jesus. 'Child, why have you treated us like this? Look, your father and I have been searching for you in great anxiety' (v. 48). I think at this point they expected an apology, but instead they get something of a ticking off as Jesus asks what frankly sounds like a pretty stupid question, 'Why were you searching for me?' (v. 49). I can imagine that Joseph would have stepped forward at this point and wanted to reply, 'Well, why do you think we were searching for you? What kind of parents would we be if we had said, "Oh, we've lost our son. Never mind, he'll probably turn up one day"?' I take comfort from the fact that despite their wonderful openness to God, Mary and Joseph are essentially very normal parents at this point.

So they listen to Jesus' reasoning, and he tells them that he had to be in his Father's house (v. 49), and again we see a normal human reaction from Mary and Joseph, for 'they did not understand what he said to them' (v. 50). I am a bit surprised by this, because Mary in particular comes over as such an insightful person in the early stories. On this occasion, however, her mother-love is so strong that she can't quite step back and understand what is really going on. No doubt she talked much with Jesus on the way home and began to understand these events and indeed treasured them in her heart (v.

51). It's a remarkable testimony to her that an experience that must have caused her so much distress actually became a treasure for her. She was coming to understand that her son was now fully aware that he was not the son of Joseph but the son of the Father in heaven, the Lord God Almighty, and therefore it was quite fitting and natural for him to be in the temple, the nearest place to his Father's home.

For Mary and Joseph this event was another part of their steep learning curve and the beginning of their letting go of Jesus and of releasing him towards the destiny that awaited him. They lost him for three days and then found him, and those three days resonate with the three days when he was later lost in the valley of death. In one sense their child had died, and he was raised up again as a man, just as he later died as a man and was raised again, having conquered death.

It seems to me that this episode is a not uncommon experience. Any parent can find that some incident happens to their child and they suddenly become aware that a little more of the child has gone and a little more of the adult has emerged. Parenting is full of the experiences of letting go of the old and embracing the new. It is also true in our relationship with Jesus. Everyone who knows about Jesus has some kind of a relationship with him. For one it may simply be the relationship of knowing him as a historical figure, whereas for another it may be knowing him as the God they worship. Whatever it is, there are likely to be times when we have to let go of one way of viewing him so that we can move to a more accurate view. For many it has been that vital change from acknowledging him as an impressive figure in history to accepting him personally as God.

For those who are Christians there can also be changes. I knew someone once who grew up in a very strict religious environment, and for her Jesus was a God who insisted on good behaviour and was like an unkind and strict teacher. This image of Jesus followed her throughout her life. She faithfully went to church and tried to do all the things that she had been told this Jesus wanted her to do. In time she reached a level of honesty to say that she could no longer worship this kind of God, and she effectively lost contact with the Jesus who had been such an oppressive figure in her life. Little by little, however, she discovered that there was 'another' Jesus who was very different: a Jesus who was compassionate, who carried the scars of his suffering and understood hers; who was more interested in listening to her than telling her how to behave; who actually loved her for who she was. It was only as she was prepared to lose that old image of Jesus that she was able to discover a much truer picture of him. Like Mary and Joseph she had to let go and then search and find him in a new way—and she continues to ponder these things in her heart.

Reflection

What is your view of Jesus? Can you think of times when you have had to let go of a false image of him so that you can make way for a more accurate image? As you reflect on your life now, is there any sense in which you need to let go of an old image of him and become open to something new?

Prayer

Help me to discover you as you really are, Lord Jesus. Give me the eyes to recognize you for who you are, not for what others say you should be, and be with me in the ponderings of my heart as I seek to know you better.

✥

Week 5

Illumination

I hate Christmas lights going up in the streets in September! I know they don't turn them on for some weeks, but it still feels as if someone is hurrying me on to winter while I, with my love for summer, am doing all I can to cling on to the last warm days and savour the light. Come mid November, however, and I am starting to get ready. The days are becoming so much shorter, and there is a real chill in the air. I have noticed that at some point during November the light changes—the sun may shine bright, but it has far less power. In our homes and offices (in the northern hemisphere) we need to have the lights on much more often and we know that winter is closing in. Against the backdrop of chilly fogs and cold nights, there comes an abundance of coloured lights in our homes and streets. I know they are artificial, and some of them are pretty lurid. They are nothing like the bright sun of a July day. But they do speak of that wonderful tendency in the human heart to find ways of celebrating with colour and light even in the darkest times of the year.

In our readings over this coming week we shall be very aware of the themes of light. We shall think about those mysterious men from the East who got caught up in the excitement of a bright light in the sky, and by the end of the week we shall be reading part of the Gospel of John, who loved the powerful symbolism of light.

In some ways I recoil from writing about light in the darkness. It can be rather hackneyed, an overused metaphor, and everyone is fed up with the over-familiar 'light at the end of the tunnel' words of encouragement. A part of me feels it would be better left alone, but no matter how badly we treat this imagery, I find I can't get away from it. The Gospel writers know this. As we survey our world, there is no doubt that too much of life seems to be lived in dark places, and we need to hear these Gospel stories again to be assured that there is a light that can reach through every darkness in the world.

Spirit of truth and love,
Life-giving, holy Dove,
Speed forth Thy flight:
Move on the water's face
Bearing the lamp of grace,
And in earth's darkest place
Let there be light![23]

❖

29 December

A star is born

In the time of King Herod, after Jesus was born in Bethlehem of Judea, wise men from the East came to Jerusalem, asking, 'Where is the child who has been born king of the Jews? For we observed his star at its rising, and have come to pay him homage.'
MATTHEW 2:1–2

For the next few days we shall look at one of the infancy stories from Matthew's Gospel, namely the coming of the Magi. By any reckoning this is a curious episode. In his first chapter, Matthew has given us a long genealogy and a very concise account of the birth of Jesus. He then gives a much more detailed account of the strange visitors from the East and the machinations of Herod to destroy Jesus.

He begins this chapter by telling us that Jesus was born in Bethlehem, and he tells this mainly for the benefit of devout Jews. This town carried great significance. The name meant 'house of bread' and was the home and city of King David (1 Samuel 16:1), and it was from the line of David that God would send the Messiah, and indeed from David's own town (see John 7:42). Hearing all this, Jewish people would have been reassured that events fitted with Old Testament prophecy. Matthew then mentions Herod, who was not a popular figure, and we shall look closer at this man in tomorrow's reading. Today we shall think about these travellers from the East whom Matthew calls 'Magi'.

Just who were they? The historian Herodotus tells us that they were a tribe of priests from the Persian Empire, the equivalent of the Levites, who were the Jewish group of priests. No one knows precisely where they came from as Matthew gives us only the vague reference to 'the East', but they possibly came from the Babylon area, that much-dreaded place where the Jews were once taken into exile following the destruction of Jerusalem by the Babylonian armies. The Magi were a very influential group in Persia, and it was they who instructed the Persian kings. They were seen as men of holiness and wisdom, and were skilled in philosophy and natural science. They also had skills to do with understanding the signs of the times and predicting events in the future, mainly through looking at the night sky and learning from the stars. They mapped the sky and studied the movement of the constellations and wondered at the amazing and delicate order of the universe. They believed that this order was directed by God, and if God should ever choose to do something different or extraordinary, he would disturb that order for a time to catch the attention of those who had eyes to see.

Thus we have a group of these wise, listening men who are on the lookout for God's signals in the heavens. One night they spotted something very different. Quite what they saw is a matter of speculation. We know that Halley's Comet was visible around 11BC, and in 7BC there was a brilliant conjunction of Saturn and Jupiter which lit up the evening sky. In the years between 5 and 2BC Sirius, the Dog Star, was also shining very brightly. Whatever it was that they saw, these Magi clearly 'heard' a message in the heavens through which they were told that in the land of the Jews a king was born and they were called to visit him. The Magi were not alone in detecting this, as the Roman writers Suetonius and Tacitus described a widespread belief that someone would arise in Judaea who would rule the world.[24] The first readers of Matthew's Gospel would therefore not have been surprised to learn that these perceptive listeners of the heavens detected such signals and wanted to find out more.

Matthew's purpose in recording this story is almost certainly to tell us something very significant about the birth of Jesus: that his coming was not just for a select few from a particular faith. Jesus was not a messiah just for the Jewish people; his significance was far wider than that. His life would have a relevance even to those from the once hostile Persian lands that had been responsible for devastating Jerusalem. Matthew was telling his readers that Jesus was a gift for the whole world, and even if you knew nothing about the Old Testament or about Jewish beliefs about the Messiah, you could still catch the sound of a new song being sung in the universe; that something truly wonderful was happening and a new order was about to come into being, one that had the potential to bring the whole world together and heal ancient divisions. Later in his Gospel, Matthew tells us that Jesus' term for this world was 'the Kingdom of Heaven' (see, for example, Matthew 13:24–52).

The fact that God chose to speak to the Magi in the language they could understand is one of the most wonderful aspects of these nativity stories. It tells us something very important about God: he wishes to communicate the good news of his son Jesus to *all* people, regardless of their faith or beliefs. It is often assumed that the good news about Jesus is really only relevant to church people and that if God is going to speak about him, then only church people will understand the language. The story about the Magi and Herod tells us that this is far from true. Herod, who is the one who should have heard the news about the Messiah, misses it completely, whereas the pagan Magi hear it perfectly. For those of us who are churchgoing Christians, this is rather a disturbing story. It implies that we in the church can quite easily miss what God is telling us about his Son, whereas those outside the church who have hearts that long for all that is good, peaceful and healing for this world may actually understand what we are too deaf to hear. But then, how many modern 'Magi' do hear the good news, make a long journey to church to worship him, but find they are rejected because they don't fit in culturally? It is a curious thing, but in this story it is the pagan astrologers who are telling the religious leaders about their Messiah.

Increasingly I am seeing a greater openness among Christians who are daring to listen to others to learn about their perspectives of Jesus. One of the most influential books on mission in recent years has been Vincent J. Donovan's *Christianity Rediscovered*. In this book the writer, working from his long experience with the Masai people, argues that true mission involves walking alongside people in their journey and becoming fellow explorers, working with the conviction that the Holy Spirit will be the guide. It's a risky journey because Christians may well have to readjust some of their views as they listen to the other. In a preface to the second edition of his book, Donovan quotes a young person's reflection on his book and sees it as very good missionary advice:

In working with young people in America, do not try to call them back to where they were, and do not try to call them to where you are, as beautiful as that place might seem to you. You must have the courage to go with them to a place that neither you nor they have ever been before.[25]

Reflection

What do you think about the quote from Vincent Donovan? How might it affect both how you listen to God and also how you share the good news with others? If you do not feel you can call yourself a Christian, have there been times when, like the Magi, you think you have picked up signals about something really important to which you need to listen? Think again about the messages that God may be conveying to you personally.

Prayer

God of Magis and monks, saints and sceptics, religious and rebellious, open our eyes and ears that we may see and hear the signals from heaven and, like those wise men of old, keep travelling until we have got your message.

⊹

30 December

There's always a Herod

When King Herod heard this, he was frightened, and all Jerusalem with him; and calling together all the chief priests and scribes of the people, he inquired of them where the Messiah was to be born. They told him, 'In Bethlehem of Judea; for so it has been written by the prophet: "And you, Bethlehem, in the land of Judah, are by no means least among the rulers of Judah; for from you shall come a ruler who is to shepherd my people Israel."' Then Herod secretly called for the wise men and learned from them the exact time when the star had appeared. Then he sent them to Bethlehem, saying, 'Go and search diligently for the child; and when you have found him, bring me word so that I may also go and pay him homage.'
MATTHEW 2:3–8

As we have already seen, the Judea into which Jesus was born was part of the colossal Roman Empire. The method Rome used to rule Judea was to put into place a king who would be under the authority of Rome and yet would also be one of the people. Thus in 40BC the Roman Senate gave Herod the title 'King of the Jews' and this Herod was to remain in power until 4BC.[26] Herod was half Jew and half Idumean (of Idumea or Edom, in Western Asia, a country often at war with Israel). Devout Jews never forgot this half-pagan side and did not consider him to be a proper Jew. He caused great offence to the Jewish people by building temples to pagan deities. Herod's achievements included keeping the peace in Judea during his time and engaging in serious rebuilding work in Jerusalem, including the temple. To fund these building projects, both in Judaea and in other parts of the Roman Empire, he had to keep on extracting money from his people through harsh taxation. From time to time he showed kindness and compassion to his people, but in the main he was a distant man who was obsessed with wealth and splendour, as well as intensely suspicious and jealous.

He very easily became suspicious of anyone whom he felt might weaken his power and during his reign he murdered his wife, his three sons, his mother-in-law, his brother-in-law, his uncle and countless others whom he viewed as a threat to his position. It is entirely consistent with his character, then, that he should receive the news from the Magi with great suspicion. Matthew tells us that Herod was frightened and 'all Jerusalem with him' (v. 3). The people would have been desperately anxious about how Herod would respond to this news, knowing of the violence in his character. Herod must have been infuriated that these foreigners came casually into his land, asking where the 'King of the Jews' was to be born. As far as Herod was concerned, there was only one King of the Jews and no room for another. His paranoid disposition meant that he could only interpret this as a plot to overthrow him. But he needed more information, so he got together his chief priests and scribes to work out the likely location of this usurper. He gleaned from them that the Messiah was to be born in Bethlehem, so he concluded that if someone was purporting to be the Messiah and an alternative King of the Jews, it was likely that they were plotting to do so in Bethlehem. We get the impression that at this point he was presenting himself as very respectful of these foreign visitors and ironically he invited them to return to him to let him know the news so he might then 'go and pay him homage' (in other words, murder him). The Magi, being wise and perceptive people, no doubt had some misgivings about Herod, which later gave them an openness to receiving a warning dream (v. 12), instructing them not to return to tell Herod about the baby.

For those of us who are familiar with this story, we already feel an icy chill because we know that Herod will soon unleash his terrible anger in the direction of innocent children. The first readers, even though they did not know what was coming, knew enough about Herod to be anxious. So far in the story, Jesus has been born safely in Bethlehem, which is exactly where he was supposed to be born, and these wise men are confirming the message of the story by their journey and visit to Bethlehem. But the early reader almost certainly would have been wondering why they had to tell Herod because they would know of his likely response. It is, however, encouraging to learn a little later on in the story that the wise men were truly discerning and chose not to respond to Herod's request that was driven by his fears (v. 12).

Figures such as Herod are not uncommon as we look at the history of the nations of this world. We see unwise, insecure people somehow wheedling their way to political power and then ruling unjustly. Such people have often caused immense human suffering. And it is not just on the world scale that we see this. It can be the boss with whom you find yourself working or, sadly, church leaders who are not immune to the seductions of power and influence. Also, if we are very honest, we need to explore our own hearts, for most of us are in situations in which we exercise leadership and have influence over others in one way or another.

Herod was someone who had been entrusted with authority; his power was considerable. And yet, on hearing this news about the Messiah, we are told he was frightened (v. 3), for a raw nerve had obviously been touched. There is an unacknowledged fear within him, a doubt as to whether he is really the all-powerful king of the Jews he believes himself to be. He rushes anxiously to his aides to see what they have to say and, sure enough, they discover that there is a story of another king. This news confirms Herod's anxiety, and all that he does now is motivated by his fear, with a single purpose in mind—saving himself. He is supposed to be on the throne to watch over and protect a nation, but this act reveals that his main concern is looking after Number One.

All leaders have to face similar fears sooner or later. In Herod's case it was the emergence of a (in his view) rival king, but the threats can come in many different ways. People can question a leader's authority or competence or relational skills. In recent years much has been written on the need for leaders to develop 'emotional intelligence', a concept made popular by Daniel Goleman[27] , which encourages leaders to recognize, understand and monitor their own feelings, and identify how they affect the emotions of those they are serving. It has to be said that Herod displayed a very low level of emotional intelligence in this story! He could have acknowledged the rumblings of fear in his heart and investigated them more carefully, making sure his response to this piece of news arose from careful and prayerful consideration, rather than simply a gut reaction. If we are in any kind of leadership, it is always worth registering what it is that causes us to feel afraid and ensure that it is not our fears that are driving our decisions.

In this story it is the wise men who show true emotional intelligence. They had cause for fear and may have had some in their souls. But we see no pandering to Herod's wealth and power in the way they respond to him. They were not deceived by his apparently flattering words, but remained discerning and therefore open to the guidance of God.

When we are with people who have some authority or influence over us and whose behaviour is driven by fears and insecurity rather than by wisdom, we can all too easily join in the 'power games' they play, and it can take much courage to challenge them. The wise men did not challenge Herod and they had the freedom to walk away, back to their homelands. But we can't always do that. There may be times when we have to hold on to our integrity and work to help a leader face up to their inner fears. This can be a very difficult road, but it can enable the leader to grow into a new place of wholeness and ensure that those being led are treated more fairly.

Reflection

Where do you exercise leadership? In the home? At work? In your church? Can you think of times when you may have responded out of fear rather than wisdom? If so, how could you make changes for the future?

Prayer

Lord, you know me far better than I know myself. Please search my soul, and visit that part of me where I keep my hidden fears. Please bring such healing that I may respond to others out of love, not fear, and out of wisdom, not insecurity.

✥

Thesaurus

When they had heard the king, they set out; and there, ahead of them, went the star that they had seen at its rising, until it stopped over the place where the child was. When they saw that the star had stopped, they were overwhelmed with joy. On entering the house, they saw the child with Mary his mother; and they knelt down and paid him homage. Then, opening their treasure chests, they offered him gifts of gold, frankincense, and myrrh.

MATTHEW 2:9–11

The Magi set off, having been told by the local religious experts that Bethlehem was the right place for the arrival of the Messiah and, as expected, there was the faithful star shining down brightly on the town. Matthew tells us that the star stopped over the place where the child was. I don't think Matthew expects us to imagine a Christmas card scene of a neatly parked star in the sky, shining a spotlight on to a stable. The impression I get from the Gospel account is that whatever the sign in the heavens guiding the Magi has been, it has now done its work. It remains in the sky and carries on its course, but it no longer has significance for these wise men, who have listened to the heavens, received the message and found what they were seeking.

We are told at this point that they were overwhelmed with joy (v. 10). The Greek text literally says, 'they rejoiced with an exceeding and great joy'. Matthew is using all the superlatives he can find to convey the sheer volume of joy these men were experiencing. In some ways, I find this extraordinary. By the standards of their day, these men had travelled an enormous distance. They had visited the splendid palace of Herod and no doubt seen the magnificent temple he had built and all the other great walls and buildings. But those great sights did not give them joy. It was when they got to a much more ordinary town that they started to feel this powerful emotion.

At this point they knew that their journey had been worthwhile. They had found Bethlehem, and they had found the Messiah. They hadn't even seen him yet, but they were overwhelmed by joy, simply knowing they had found the right place. Maybe, like the shepherds, they were also rejoicing at the simplicity of the place—this was a messiah who was making his home in normal everyday life. Maybe this was what they were longing for in some way.

Matthew tells us that the Magi go into a 'house', which may suggest that the family have moved from the stable. Some have suggested that this episode might be a year or two after Jesus was born. For Mary and Joseph, it must have been an extraordinary experience. We know they were from humble origins, poor people who could only afford two doves for their sacrifice (Luke 2:24). The Magi were VIPs from another nation and were the last kind of people that Mary and Joseph imagined meeting. But they welcomed them in as friends, and as the Magi came in they saw that Mary was cradling her child, and they knelt down and worshipped him. This, we are told in Matthew 2:2, was the purpose of their visit. They had travelled miles and miles to worship this God, who was in the form of a young child on his mother's lap.

When you think about it, it must have been a quite remarkable scene: Mary, a young teenager from a poor background, tenderly holding her little son, and a group of foreign, finely-dressed men kneeling in front of her. We don't know how they expressed their worship—did they sing, pray, chant? Did they weep, laugh? Were they silent or did they speak? Something deep in their spirits told them that this was what they had been questing for all their lives. Their studying of the stars, their tracking of the constellations in the night sky, their poring over learned books, their deciphering of ancient documents, their detailed searches through almanacs of wisdom, their prayers and chants, the cries of their hearts—all these had led them to this moment and they were now at peace.

Why? Why were they so delighted, so sure, so contented? Maybe their gifts give us a clue. We don't know how many Magi there were, and it is only because they brought three gifts that people supposed there were three, each one bringing a gift. But it seems they brought three gifts because they had three specific messages to deliver. Matthew tells us that they opened their 'treasure' (v. 11), and the Greek word he uses is *thesaurus*. A thesaurus is something we usually associate with words. If you don't understand a word, you can go to a thesaurus and it will tell you about the meaning and offer you other, similar words. So the Magi open their *thesaurus*, which is in the form of three 'words' that are full of meaning.

The first gift or 'word' is gold. We don't know if they presented a nugget of gold or a golden goblet or ornament. Gold has always been considered a very precious metal, but the particular meaning of this gift was that it signified royalty. The Magi had already told Herod that they were searching for the King of the Jews (v. 2). Their gift tells us that they knew they had found their king, but as the events of the Gospel unfold, we discover that Jesus is not like normal kings, who reign over nations and territories. He was a king of a very different sort of kingdom. In his discussion about politics with Pontius Pilate, he makes clear that his kingdom is 'not from this world' (John 18:36). Matthew's Gospel is full of Jesus' teaching about his kingdom, and he spells out clearly in the Sermon on the Mount what kind of a kingdom his is (Matthew 5—7). Somehow I suspect that those Magi, kneeling in that simple home, knew what kind of king he was to be.

The second gift is frankincense. This was incense made from the resin of terebinth trees, which are found in the part of the world from which the Magi travelled. It was one ingredient of the holy anointing oil as described in Exodus 30:34 and was used by priests in various offerings. The meaning of this gift therefore is to do with Jesus' priestly ministry. Very simply, in the Bible the priest's role was to be an intermediary between the people and God: they would take the prayers of the people and offer them to God, and they would take the blessings of God and offer them to the people. The Magi could see that this little child would be a priest *par excellence*, one who would bring humans and God together.

The third gift is myrrh, and this was the strangest of the gifts, because myrrh was what was used to embalm dead bodies. Nicodemus took a large quantity of myrrh to the tomb for the embalming of Jesus' body after his death on the cross (John 19:39). It was as if the Magi had brought Jesus a funeral shroud; it would have instantly spoken to his family about death and would have seemed a rather ominous gift. The 'word' of this gift was clear—here was a king-priest who would suffer death. It makes us think of the old prophet Simeon, who foretold to Mary that a sword would pierce her heart (Luke 2:35), indicating that there was sorrow mixed in with this message of joy. It seems an uncomfortable paradox that men so full of delight should be presenting a gift that spoke about death. How much did they know of the story? Had they pondered so deeply that they actually glimpsed an insight which was not just about the death of this king, but about the fact that this king would conquer death itself? We shall never know, but we do know there were clues in this *thesaurus* for those with ears to hear.

Some words are very difficult to understand or explain and we need the help of a thesaurus. Mary and Joseph must have treasured the thesaurus that the Magi left with them as a way of helping them to understand all that was happening. In our lives there will always be some unsolved puzzles, words we don't understand and jokes we don't get. Then we may be visited by someone who brings with them some kind of thesaurus. It might be a book that suddenly helps us to make sense of something; it might be a TV programme or a film or a sermon or a song; it might be the way we see light falling on water or the flight of a flock of geese in an autumn sky. These are moments when something becomes clear—we 'get it', and when we do, it can become a treasure. Quite a lot of life is about the willingness to live with the unsolved and unclear and yet wait patiently for a light from the star to reach us. Perhaps the key is to follow the example of those Magi—always being on the lookout for signs, full of expectation and also full of hope.

Reflection

What is unsolved for you at the moment? What has happened or is happening in your life that you do not understand? Spend some time in quiet reflection—can you get any sense of where or how you need to journey to make your discovery?

Prayer

God of the questing Magi, take me on a journey of discovery and give me eyes to see starlight at night and ears to hear whispers by day and a heart that is open to experiencing exceeding and great joy.

✤

1 January

The intensity of darkness

And having been warned in a dream not to return to Herod, they [the Magi] left for their own country by another road. Now after they had left, an angel of the Lord appeared to Joseph in a dream and said, 'Get up, take the child and his mother, and flee to Egypt, and remain there until I tell you; for Herod is about to search for the child, to destroy him.' Then Joseph got up, took the child and his mother by night, and went to Egypt, and remained there until the death of Herod. This was to fulfil what had been spoken by the Lord through the prophet, 'Out of Egypt I have called my son.' When Herod saw that he had been tricked by the wise men, he was infuriated, and he sent and killed all the children in and around Bethlehem who were two years old or under, according to the time that he had learned from the wise men. Then was fulfilled what had been spoken through the prophet Jeremiah: 'A voice was heard in Ramah, wailing and loud lamentation, Rachel weeping for her children; she refused to be consoled, because they are no more.'

MATTHEW 2:12–18

Following the story of the Magi, we come to a tale that horribly stains the nativity stories. The Church traditionally remembers this event on 28 December. In recent weeks we have travelled with good and faithful people—Mary, Joseph, Elizabeth, Zechariah, Simeon, Anna and the Magi. We have certainly seen some suffering in our stories and encountered the effects of poverty. But here in this story, we are faced with sheer evil and brutality. It is all the worse because Herod, the ruler of the Jews, should be the person at the forefront of the crowd welcoming the coming Messiah and bringing gifts to honour the newborn king. That thought doesn't even enter his head.

Matthew tells us that Herod is furious, for these Magi have disobeyed him (v. 16). He had insisted that they come back to him after visiting this Messiah that they were so excited about. His plan was to get a precise location so that he could eliminate this potential threat to his crown. No doubt he would have killed the Magi as well, to crush any rebellious rumours. But the Magi have been listening. We have seen how skilled they had been at listening to the world of the stars and planets (the outer world). They had also reflected deeply on the meaning of this newborn king. They detected Herod's jealousy and fear behind his lies. We also have evidence that they are excellent listeners to their own hearts (the inner world), specifically through the language of dreams, and because they are alert in this way, they receive the message that it would be dangerous to return to Herod. They depart on another route, avoiding any contact with Herod or his soldiers.

Herod now feels he has been made to look foolish and has been humiliated by these Magi who have escaped. He can't do much about them once they are over the border, but he can do something about this 'King of the Jews' that they claimed to have found. He does not know where the house is, but he knows it was in Bethlehem, and thus he sends his soldiers out to slaughter all the toddlers in and around the town. We know that Herod was bloodthirsty even by the standards of his day, but this act of violence toward innocent children was particularly horrendous. Bethlehem was not a big town, so the number of slain may not have been that high. However, even one murdered child would be shocking and the people of that town and neighbourhood would have felt the pain intensely. We don't know how much they knew about the story of Jesus. Maybe the shepherds had told lots of people and Mary, Joseph and Jesus were well known. Or was it that very few knew the prophecies about this little child? Certainly the visit of the Magi must have caused a bit of a stir. But in the main, most of these people must have felt they were caught up in one of Herod's grotesque demonstrations of power, and they were mere pawns in his hands.

As Matthew relates this story, his way of trying to make sense of it and provide some kind of consolation is to look back to an ancient story. He quotes from the prophet Jeremiah (31:15) about weeping in Ramah, a town about five miles north of Jerusalem. It was one of the towns through which the defeated people of Jerusalem passed as captives on their way to exile in Babylon. The weeping heard in Bethlehem, says Matthew, is like the weeping heard all those years ago, when the people of God were led away wounded, hurt and torn from their beloved homeland, their lives completely ruined. Matthew quotes also the second part of the Jeremiah verse which compares the weeping to that of Rachel (Jacob's favourite wife—see Genesis 29:30), who grieved so deeply for her lost children that she could not be comforted. In using this verse, Matthew is being both prophetic and pastoral. He knows that all who read this story will feel deeply for the grieving families, and so he leads us to Rachel, one of the great mothers of faith in Israel, and reminds us that we are in good company. It's almost a gesture saying, 'It's all right to mourn.' If we know people have been there before us and come through, we are given some strength to carry on.

The use of the verse from Jeremiah to connect this episode to the journey of the exiles is prophetic. For the families grieving the loss of their little ones, their world was completely shattered. But the context of Jeremiah 31 is all about hope. The chapter has the following words in verse 2: 'The people who survived the sword found grace in the wilderness,' and there follows much about God's healing love. By referring us to this passage and reminding us of the exile, Matthew is declaring that not even exile is completely disastrous, because God can do extraordinary things in the wilderness of grief and suffering and bring about a renewal of hope. The very next verses after the reference to Rachel's weeping read, 'They shall come back from the land of the enemy; there is hope for your future, says the Lord: your children shall come back to their own country' (Jeremiah 31:16–17).

Had Joseph not been a good listener, then he and Mary would have been among the grieving parents. But at the start of this story, we read that he had a dream in which he heard an angel calling him to take Mary and Jesus to Egypt, well out of harm's way. Thus, right at the start of his life, Jesus becomes a refugee, fleeing a tyrant who is obsessed with his destruction. There were many Jews living in Egypt and it was an obvious place to go to seek safety. So Jesus takes the journey that his ancestors took: he went down to Egypt for a time, before returning through the desert to the Promised Land. Again, Matthew, who loves to connect all this with Old Testament prophecy, reminds us of the prophecy in Hosea (11:1) that refers to God's calling his son up out of Egypt.

Matthew's intention in telling this episode is to make very clear just how vulnerable the young Jesus was in this world, and show the destructive powers of evil that were on the prowl to eliminate him. But he was protected by those who were prepared to listen to God and to adapt their plans accordingly. While we rejoice at the fact that Jesus was spared, we can't help our joy being tempered by the sad fate suffered by the other children. All untimely death is hard to take, and the death of children is the worst, particularly when it is the result of deliberate cruelty. From time to time we read terrible accounts of children being shot by deranged gunmen, or caught up in bomb blasts in violent parts of the world. Add to those the vast numbers who die of disease and starvation because we cannot share our resources fairly. Today's story does not offer a slick and easy answer to that problem, but there is a point of comfort for us in knowing that God in his incarnation chose to identify himself with defenceless and suffering children. Rachel still continues to grieve and weep over this world where there is too much infant suffering, but this story tells us that it is a weeping that is heard in the chambers of heaven. It is also a story that delivers a word of hope to those going through hard times, that fresh pools of grace can be found in the wilderness.

Reflection

Today's Bible passage does not make for comfortable reading. What do you do with your feelings when you hear stories of children who suffer? Are you able to turn your feelings into prayer? Even if your prayer doesn't get beyond expressing sorrow and anger, can you make a start?

Prayer

Lord, when I have no words, hear the thoughts of my heart, the stirrings of my spirit and the tears that fall from my eyes, that I may find your pools of grace in the wilderness places.

✢

2 January

Light, part 1

In the beginning was the Word, and the Word was with God, and the Word was God. He was in the beginning with God. All things came into being through him, and without him not one thing came into being. What has come into being in him was life, and the life was the light of all people. The light shines in the darkness, and the darkness did not overcome it.
JOHN 1:1–5

We have looked at Luke and Matthew's account of the coming of Jesus into this world. They give straightforward, coherent accounts, with easy-to-follow narratives. John is not so easy! In the next four days we shall look at the opening verses to his Gospel, and as we shall see he takes an entirely different approach to both Matthew and Luke. Almost certainly he would have known about the nativity stories, but he chooses to ignore them and come at it all from a very different angle.

In a rather stark way, John begins his account of the life of Jesus with the powerful words, 'In the beginning was the Word.' That 'In the beginning' would remind Jewish readers of the opening verses of Genesis, and they would be taken right back to the creation of the world, when, according to the writer of Genesis, all life proceeded from God speaking his words of command, 'Let there be light... Let there be a dome in the midst of the waters...' and so on (Genesis 1:1–26). The Jewish readers would know that the word of God was indeed powerful, and they would agree that in the beginning there was indeed the word: God spoke and things happened. They would be in complete agreement with John as they read this account and he declared that the Word was with God and that all things came into being through him. But the Gospel writer was not just writing to faithful Jews; he was also writing to the Greek world, where many people knew little about Judaism. It was no help to them if he did the same as Matthew and quoted lots of Old Testament scripture, because they did not know it. Nor would it be any good starting his story in Bethlehem, because no one in the Greek world would know where that was or see the significance of it. They knew nothing of those ancient prophecies of a virgin who would conceive and bear a child who would be the Messiah.

What people in the Greek world *did* know about was the 'Word', or *Logos*, to give the Greek word. Now at this point most writers on this Gospel passage would write several chapters on what the Greeks understood by 'Word', but I shall spare you that and cut quite a number of corners by saying that 'Word' used like this meant a divine force to do with wisdom and reason and was a way of talking about God. Even if we don't fully understand the Greek way of looking at it, what we can grasp is that John is attempting to put this extraordinary and wonderful story into a language that both Jews and Greeks could understand. He was trying to be bilingual, which was no easy feat with two different cultures and world views. He must have spent hours and hours crafting those opening verses, praying and hoping that his words would in some way convey the earth-shattering news that God had come to this world as one of us.

Having introduced God as 'Word', John then brings in one of his other favourite themes: light. For the Jew this is familiar territory. In the story of creation, described in Genesis 1, light is the first thing that God creates. What is interesting about that account is that light is created before the sun. It seems to me that the writer of Genesis wanted us to understand that there is a light that is more than sunlight. It is a light of a more spiritual type—a light that we all need to live but that does not go out when the sun goes down; a light that exists both on earth and in heaven. So John takes up this type of light in his opening verses as he proclaims that the Word is responsible for producing life and this life is a light (in the Genesis sense) for *all* people. John is keen to emphasize that this light is for everyone, not just the Jewish people. He loves this theme of light, and it crops up 21 times in his Gospel. Twice Jesus calls himself the 'light of the world' (John 8:12 and 9:5) and his light can be in people (11:10) so that they can become 'children of light' (12:36). A vital piece of the good news of John's story is that Jesus is one who comes to bring this kind of light to all who will receive it.

Just as John is very aware of this light, he is also aware that the world has many areas of darkness. Thus, he records Jesus' declaring that those who follow his light will never walk in darkness (8:12) and of course John is very keen to point out that on the day of the resurrection of Jesus, Mary comes to the tomb 'while it was still dark' (20:1). He shows that Jesus rose from the dead in the dark hours of the night as a sure sign that the power of the resurrection has scattered the darkness of this world.

The themes of light and darkness have always been a source of fascination to many people. I've been writing this book over the course of a year, and living with this theme of hope has made me acutely aware of the light and darkness at particular times of the year. I've been made aware again how much I need the light, how grumpy I get when there is not enough in the winter, and how much I love the long evenings and still feel a thrill when I'm driving back from a meeting at 10.30pm and I draw into a lay-by and gaze in amazement over Derbyshire fields, still visible under a luminous sky. This is not the light John is talking about, of course. He is writing about something less literal and more spiritual. I find it hard to describe it, but I know I recognize it when I encounter it. An example is a song by The Blind Boys of Alabama. This is a well-known and long established black band which, as their name suggests, is made up of blind singers. There is something very special about listening to their song 'There will be a Light', which they sing with Ben Harper.[28] The words have a beautiful simplicity, each verse ending with the refrain, 'There will be a light', which is sung with gentleness and conviction and wonderful harmonies. For these blind men, my wonder at long summer evenings over Derbyshire fields has little significance. They have knowledge of a light that has nothing to do with the sun, but everything to do with living fully in this world despite the lack of eyesight. It is to do with an instinct about light and darkness and an assurance that light is and will be theirs.

Yesterday we read about the appalling darkness in Herod, whose orders brought about the death of innocent children. Sometimes when we read the national and international news stories, we can be tempted to think that the darkness will overcome the light, and when we are tempted to believe that, this verse from the opening of John's Gospel is the one to go back to and declare again, 'The darkness will not overcome it.' After all, if you light a match in the darkness, the light always wins, no matter how great the darkness and how small the match. That is language understood by Jew, Greek and all humanity.

Reflection

What do you think this type of light is? How would you try to describe it? Have you seen examples of this light shining in the darkness?

Prayer

There will be a light. There will be a light. There will be a light.

✥

Light, part 2

There was a man sent from God, whose name was John. He came as a witness to testify to the light, so that all might believe through him. He himself was not the light, but he came to testify to the light. The true light, which enlightens everyone, was coming into the world.

JOHN 1:6–9

It is said that this prologue to John's Gospel is like an overture. It picks up the tunes that appear in the main work and works them together as an introduction. In these mysterious verses John introduces us to four themes that recur throughout his Gospel: light, life, glory and grace. We shall explore each theme a little for our four final readings, although the themes are so closely connected that we may find we weave in and out of them all as we go on. In fact, reading these verses feels in some way like entering new and very different waters from those of Matthew and Luke, who provided clear and definite markers to steer us. John moves in and out between the ethereal and the practical; he introduces us to the very human John the Baptist while at the same time explaining to us about this Word made flesh; he talks about flesh and blood at the same time as talking about light and glory.

We saw yesterday that John starts his Gospel at the beginning of all things and declares that the unconquered light has come into the world. In today's reading he develops this theme of light. When I read these opening verses of John's Gospel, I am reminded of the story of Narnia, *The Voyage of the Dawn Treader* by C.S. Lewis. Written as a children's book, it is typically full of humour and adventure but towards the end it becomes increasingly mystical. In this book, two of the heroes of *The Lion, the Witch and the Wardrobe*, Lucy and Edmund, are once again drawn into Narnia, this time with their cousin Eustace. They find themselves on board the ship *Dawn Treader*, which is captained by King Caspian, who has undertaken a quest to find the seven lost Lords of Narnia. They are accompanied on their travels by the indomitable talking mouse Reepicheep. During the voyage they manage to find all seven Lords on various islands. Two of them are dead, two of them are alive, and three of them are in a deep enchanted sleep on the Island of the Star. The only way to awaken them is to sail to the edge of the world and leave behind one member of the crew, which turns out to be Reepicheep. The penultimate chapter is called 'The Wonders of the Last Sea', and those on board the ship begin to feel they are entering a whole new world, one in which they feel themselves to be more alive than they have ever been.

At one point they realize that the water around the ship is no longer seawater but water of a quite different type:

'It—it's like light more than anything else,' said Caspian.

'That is what it is,' said Reepicheep. 'Drinkable light. We must be very near the end of the world now.'

There was a moment's silence and then Lucy knelt down on the deck and drank from the bucket.

'It's the loveliest thing I have ever tasted,' she said with a kind of gasp. 'But oh—it's strong. We shan't need to eat anything now.'

And one by one everybody on board drank. And for a long time they were silent... Now, the light grew no less—if anything it increased—but they could bear it. They could look straight up at the sun without blinking. They could see more light than they had ever seen before. And the deck and the sail and their own faces and bodies became brighter and brighter and every rope shone. And next morning, when the sun rose, now five or six times its old size, they stared hard into it and could see the very feathers of the birds that came flying from it.[29]

To me, the opening verses from John's Gospel have the same feel as this Narnian story. John is inviting us to explore a new world, which has a kind of drinkable light. I think he would have liked this idea, as water is another of his favourite themes that he introduces through the ministry of John the Baptist, which is characterized by water (1:26). The Baptist is introduced to us as a witness to the light. Eugene Peterson in his paraphrase of the Bible (THE MESSAGE) translates this as John being sent by God 'to point the way to the Life-Light' (1:6). This was John's God-given task. It is as if his job was to get us on board the *Dawn Treader* and lead us out to sea to taste the drinkable light and to have a strength of eyesight we have never had before, to catch a vision of things we didn't think existed.

This Gospel writer is very keen to explain that this light is available to everyone. It is a true light to enlighten everyone (v. 9), not just a favoured few. But what exactly does this light mean? Well, of course John expects his readers to move on into his book to discover more about this, and as we saw yesterday, the theme of light often occurs in the pages of his Gospel. A high point is when he records Jesus' declaring himself as the light: 'I have come as light into the world, so that everyone who believes in me should not remain in the darkness' (12:46). It's a theme that keeps coming back, almost as if John is nagging us about it. Why would he go on about it? What makes you go on about something again and again? What is so important that you keep repeating yourself?

There are experiences in life that are so profound that you have to go over them many times. For example, what were you doing on 31 August 1997? And where were you on 11 September 2001? I doubt you had to think long before you remembered the tragic death of Princess Diana in a Paris tunnel, or saw in your mind's eye yet again the jet plane hitting that tall office block in New York City on a clear September morning. These images are impressed on our minds because millions of us shared in shock at the untimely death of someone we felt we knew and loved and who symbolized so much (in the case of Diana), and millions of us felt that sense of horror at the 9/11 atrocities and imagined what we would have done if we had been in that office block and what phone calls we would have made. These are dates we all remember, but there are dates you will personally remember as well—news of a fatal accident, a lab report from the hospital, the curtain at the crematorium—moments that you may have described again and again. We all have such moments in our lives when terrible things have happened to us personally, when we have been afraid and afflicted with grief, loneliness and other life experiences that feel very dark.

It is this world that John has in mind—the world where dark things happen too often to too many people. Don't despair, says John. Go back to the words of that man by the river all those years ago. He spoke about a light that enlightens everyone, even the one who is experiencing the deepest darkness. Go back and listen to that message again. Listen to it again and again, day after day. There is enough for every darkness that afflicts this world. Let this light sink into you and learn how to drink regularly from that light, which will be living water for you. Then, when darkness engulfs you, you'll be prepared. You'll have a reserve of the light of Christ who has come into your world, and no darkness will overcome that.

Reflection

What darkness are you aware of today, either in your life or in the world? Imagine how the light of Jesus might shine into that darkness. Spend a while reflecting on the difference that would make.

Prayer

Visit then this soul of mine,
Pierce the gloom of sin and grief;
Fill me, radiancy divine,
Scatter all my unbelief;
More and more thyself display,
Shining to the perfect day.[30]

✢

4 January

Life

He was in the world, and the world came into being through him; yet the world did not know him. He came to what was his own, and his own people did not accept him. But to all who received him, who believed in his name, he gave power to become children of God, who were born, not of blood or of the will of the flesh or of the will of man, but of God.

JOHN 1:10–13

In today's reading, the Gospel writer tells us that this Word, this extraordinary divine force of reason, this expression of God, this communication of God that was involved in the creation of all things at the beginning, this brilliant light for all people, came to be one of us. Then, as with the Genesis story, we meet with tragedy almost as soon as the story gets underway. He came to his own people, his own family, but far from running to him with open arms, putting out the bunting and opening the champagne, they 'did not accept him' (v. 11). John puts it starkly and without comment. He is referring to the people of faith, the descendents of Abraham who, year after year, had longed for the Messiah to come, had prayed for him, told stories about him, prepared for his arrival. But they did not accept him. Although many did accept him, the leaders stubbornly refused to recognize Jesus as the Messiah. We know that some, like Nicodemus and Joseph of Arimathea, loved him and welcomed him, but generally the leaders—both religious and secular—rejected him. He would not conform to the kind of messiah they wanted, one that would suit their own ends and ambitions. Jesus challenged them far too much. He was an uncomfortable messiah—too uncomfortable. He did unfortunate things like turning over the tables in the temple and arguing with the Pharisees. He sided with the poor and spent time with disreputable people. He made himself ritually unclean by touching lepers and eating at the homes of tax collectors; in the opinion of most of the religious leaders, Jesus really could not be anything to do with God.

John does not dwell on this, however. He moves straight to the positive: for those who *did* receive Jesus, he gave power. For the vast majority of the people of first-century Palestine, power was a very scarce commodity. Pontius Pilate and the Roman legions had power; Herod in his palace had a great deal of power; the Pharisees and Sadducees had a lot of influence and therefore power. For the great majority, though, life was more about coping with those who had power over them. There was no European Courts of Human Rights to protect you, no trade unions, no ombudsmen and no affordable lawyers, so the news that power was on offer was certainly interesting. The news that it was God who was offering this power was more interesting still. But the news that this was empowerment to become a *child* would have been a bit puzzling, for in that culture a child had no rights at all. Already there is a hint here about the alternative nature of the Kingdom of God.

John returns to this child theme again in chapter 3, in the famous discussion between Jesus and Nicodemus, where Jesus speaks to the wise, sophisticated religious elder telling him that he has to be 'born again' (3:7). This is a shock to Nicodemus, who struggles to understand the concept. He is being introduced to the good news that the life that God gives is so radically different from anything this world offers that it is like being born anew. It is literally a gift of new life. Nicodemus would have perhaps preferred something a little more sophisticated, perhaps a nice training manual that an intelligent man like him could have read quickly. Then he could become a tutor in Jesus' academy, becoming a useful and rather well-respected member of staff. But here he is, talking to Jesus at night time (remember John's interest in light and darkness), hearing that he has to become a baby, and every now and again hearing laughter drifting over from some uncouth fishermen, who are apparently Jesus' current team of tutors. Even so, it doesn't put Nicodemus off, because he has caught the scent of something that smells like the kind of life of which he has long dreamed. He is prepared to lose almost everything in order to gain this thing of great worth. It is for him the pearl of great value (Matthew 13:45–46), and if he must become an infant in order to receive it, then so be it.

This message about becoming a child of God has various aspects to it. On the one hand, there is the strong and wonderfully affirming news that we have a place of belonging. In a world of so much division and family breakdown, this is therapeutic news indeed. But there is also a bit of a Nicodemus in us which is not altogether sure about going back to childhood again. It sounds risky. We have become mature adults and we have 'put an end to childish ways' (1 Corinthians 13:11). And yet to receive Jesus means we receive his power to become a child, and it will mean looking at those aspects of childhood that perhaps we jettisoned a bit too freely.

Frederick Buechner's *Telling the Truth* explores the Gospel as tragedy, comedy and fairy tale. In his section on the fairy tale, he spends some time discussing the well-known story, *The Wizard of Oz*, and he argues that this fails as a fairy tale because in the end Dorothy and her three companions discover that the wizard has in fact no magic at all—he is just a humbug. Dorothy and her companions have found what they have been searching for (heart, brains, courage and the route home), not because of magic, but by a recognition that they already had those things. Buechner says that the wizard is like a skilled psychotherapist who has helped them to make an inner adjustment so that they are better equipped to deal with their world, 'but he is not able to open up for them or inside of them a world of transcendence and joy because although he is a very good man, he is not really a wizard at all.'[31] A fairy story, on the other hand, opens us to worlds beyond our world:

No matter how forgotten and neglected, there is a child in all of us who is not just willing to believe in the possibility that maybe fairy tales are true after all but who is to some degree in touch with that truth. You pull the shade on the snow falling, white on white, and the child comes to life for a moment. There is a fragrance in the air, a certain passage of a song, an old photograph falling out from the pages of a book, the sound of somebody's voice in the hall that makes your heart leap and your eyes fill with tears. Who can say when or how it will be that something easters up out of the dimness to remind us of a time before we were born and after we will die?[32]

Of course Buechner is not advocating that we become naïve and gullible, but that we rediscover that openness which children have to wonder, imagine, believe and trust. Sometimes the only way to find a place of hope is to 'change and become like children' (Matthew 18:3). It is this kind of childishness that enables us to catch glimpses of the workings of the Kingdom of God.

Reflection

Thinking of the story of Nicodemus (John 3:1–21), how would you feel if Jesus said to you, 'You must be born again'? What would that mean for you? What bit of you as a child would you like to recapture, to help you to catch glimpses of the Kingdom of God?

Prayer

Holy Spirit of God, come to the child in me and cause long lost hopes to easter up in my soul today.

Week 6

Hope

We are almost at the end of our readings. If you started on 1 December and have been following this each day through the Advent and Christmas season, then you will be ending on 6 January, the 'twelfth day of Christmas', which is the also feast of Epiphany. Your journey with these readings will end on the festival day that celebrates the 'shining forth' of God to humankind in human form, in the person of Jesus.

We shall stay with John's Gospel for these last two readings, bringing to a close for exploration of the themes of hope built around the Christmas stories. For those reading during the midwinter weeks of the northern hemisphere, you will now be very aware of the long nights, and the pale light of the day, and it will probably be cold. I shall most likely be heading down to my paper shop wrapped in my coat and scarf and have my chat to Terry and Emily, who will do their usual job of cheering me up with their warmth and welcome. I may remind Terry of the comment he made to me that fine June day and I suspect we will discover that chuckle which comes from an assurance within us that even if it is a long winter, it is only a matter of time before the light returns. The chuckle will be a little moment of hope, one of many that carry us through our winters.

Some years ago I came across a poem by the Russian poet, Yunna Morits, called 'Bad Weather in Dickson Bay'. It is a graphic description of a cold Arctic landscape and with the skill of the poet, she enables us to feel the cold and the desolation of this place that has been battered by bad weather, and you start to feel the 'dove-grey soaking mist' enshrouding your own soul, until she writes the lines,

I live on a frozen shore
But in some secluded corner of the heart
I always keep hope. [33]

No matter how frozen the shoreline, we all need to have some secluded corners of our hearts where hope can be stored.

❖

5 January

Glory

And the Word became flesh and lived among us, and we have seen his glory, the glory as of a father's only son, full of grace and truth. (John testified to him and cried out, 'This was he of whom I said, "He who comes after me ranks ahead of me because he was before me."')
JOHN 1:14–15

Having introduced the theme of light, John now returns to this 'Word'. He launched his Gospel with his Genesis-like declaration—'In the beginning was the Word'—using language that would have been familiar to the various cultures that would be reading his book. 'Word' is essentially a term to do with communication, so we are getting the message that God is interested in communicating with his creation—he wants to 'have a word' with us. So how does he do it? John said he did it primarily by becoming flesh and living among us. As Peterson puts it in his translation of verse 14, 'The Word became flesh and blood, and moved into the neighbourhood' (*THE MESSAGE*). This is not humans struggling with complex maps of religious rules and ethical codes to find their way to God; this is God making his way to our neighbourhoods.

If a famous celebrity bought a house in my road, I am sure I'd soon hear talk of it, and no doubt I and the other neighbours in the road would be on the lookout for the sign of that posh car in the drive and other evidence of the glorious life we have read about in our celebrity gossip magazines. We would be rather impressed that they chose *our* road. We would have expected wealthy and famous people like them to live in far posher roads. They can't be too bad, if they want to live here. We'd be rather excited the first time we saw them, and there might come a time when we would bump into them on the pavement. What would we talk about? Who knows, they may ask us around for a drink and get to like us. We may become friends. We could say to our lesser friends, 'We've been round to *their* house.' Little by little their glory would pass to us and we might become the people that others want to get to know.

As humans, we are interested in glory, but most of our experience of glory is what we see in the world around us. It is the celebrities, the winners and the wealthy that 'get the glory'. The majority of us view them at a distance. There is another kind of glory, and this is what John is introducing us to here. God in Jesus has moved into the neighbourhood. As humans, we are naturally inquisitive. What does God look like? What does he drive? What does he wear? Where does he shop? What programmes does he watch? But none of that is important to this God who has moved into the neighbourhood, because the confusing thing is that he looks very much like one of us. In fact, you'd be very hard-pushed to notice the difference. Yet there is a glory, says John, for it is the glory 'as of a father's only son' (v. 14). That is the literal translation. The glory is that honour, delight and esteem a father has for his only child. This glory comes not from the adulation of the masses, but from the delight of the one. It expresses itself not in flashy cars, famous friends, big houses and expensive suits, but in 'grace and truth'—simple qualities of kindness and honesty.

What is all the excitement about then? A clue to what John means can be found later in chapter 12 of his Gospel—if you have time, take a look at it. This chapter is about Jesus' entering Jerusalem in triumph and then discussing his suffering and his death. In 12:23 he says, 'The hour has come for the Son of Man to be glorified,' and he explains this by saying that a grain of wheat has to fall into the ground and die if it is to become truly fruitful. It is a weighty and sad passage, full of anticipation of his suffering and death. In the midst of it, he cries out, 'Father, glorify your name,' to which an answer comes from heaven, 'I have glorified it, and I will glorify it again' (v. 28). If you read on in that chapter you will see that once again John brings in the themes of light and darkness.

There's much that could be said on the theme of glory in John's Gospel, for it is certainly a very profound one, but we can touch on it only briefly today. Let's simply take hold of that little insight from John 12, where we see that the glory being spoken of is not so much the glitz and glamour of our celebrity-obsessed world, but something quite different: it is a glory to do with a relationship between a father and a son, and it is a glory to do with suffering and self-giving, like the dying of a seed in the ground so that something better can be produced.

There is something both comforting and disturbing here. The comforting part is that when Jesus came to earth as a human, he did it without the artificial trappings of worldly glory that would have confined him to touching the lives of a privileged few. Instead, wonderfully, he connected with the lives of ordinary people. The disturbing part is this note of suffering and dying. What kind of glory is it when you are being whipped by sniggering soldiers, staggering down narrow streets with a cross on your back and dying in front of mocking crowds? It is a glory that it needs a certain kind of eyesight to see. Those who wanted Jesus to be a god who would essentially pander to their needs and make life more comfortable for them were going to be constantly disappointed. Those who wanted to be a kind of agent for the celebrity, effectively organizing God to suit their ends, would discover that Jesus was not one to be manipulated in any way. But those who were yearning for real justice and healing in a broken world would find a glory in this Messiah that would make sense. Those who understood little about the rules that so obsessed the religious authorities, yet who longed for God to touch their hitherto unnoticed lives, would find glory in this Son of Man who knew so well what human suffering was about. Added to this, there is a note of hope, because although many of the references to glory in John's Gospel are to do with the suffering of Jesus and the cross, it is all in the context of the seed's falling into the ground so that something far greater can be achieved. The cross was not the end of the story: the cross marked the point at which the seed was planted. The resurrection marked the point when a far more wonderful plant was emerging to transform the entire world.

As I have been thinking of this theme of glory as described by John, I find myself recalling the story of Maximilian Kolbe. He was the son of a Polish family, born in 1894, who became a Franciscan friar. As a young man he studied philosophy, theology, mathematics and physics in Rome, and he took a great interest in astrophysics and the prospect of space flight. After doctorates in philosophy and theology, and ordination as a priest, he taught in monasteries and seminaries, was involved in radio work and led a series of missions to Japan.

During the Second World War, he provided shelter to refugees, including 2,000 Jews whom he hid from Nazi persecution in his friary in Poland. On 17 February 1941 he was arrested by the Gestapo and later transferred to Auschwitz. In July 1941 a man from Kolbe's barrack had vanished, and the camp commander picked ten men from the same barrack to be starved to death to deter further escape attempts. When one of the selected men cried out in despair, lamenting his family, Kolbe volunteered to take his place. During the time in the punishment cell, Maximilian led the men in songs and prayer. After three weeks of dehydration and starvation, he was still alive, astonishing the guards. Though weak, he had comforted every one of the nine companions in his cell, and he continued to sing hymns and say prayers. Finally, he was executed with an injection of carbolic acid, dying on 14 August. The guard who witnessed his death said he found Father Kolbe 'still seated, propped up against the corner, his head slightly to one side, his eyes wide open and fixed on one point. As if in ecstasy, his face was serene and radiant.'[34]

It is this kind of glory that shines out in our world. Maximilian Kolbe could have had a very distinguished career full of worldly glory but instead chose a different path, one that was to lead to his untimely death. And yet, the power of God's love revealed in that cell still continues to change people's lives as the story is told across the nations.

Reflection

Spend a few moments thinking about the story of Maximilian Kolbe. Are there other people you have known or read about who have helped you understand something of this type of glory?

Prayer

Lord Jesus, move into the neighbourhood of my life, and help me to have the eyes to see the signs of your glory and the will to follow your example.

✤

6 January

Grace

From his fullness we have all received, grace upon grace. The law indeed was given through Moses; grace and truth came through Jesus Christ. No one has ever seen God. It is God the only Son, who is close to the Father's heart, who has made him known.

JOHN 1:16–18

As I handle this prologue of John's Gospel, I feel I am holding a highly valuable piece of papyrus that is like a mysterious map which, if we could fully understand it, would lead us to the treasure we long for. What happens to you when you read these phrases? Imagine that old man in the first century, in the evening of his life, writing his Gospel on parchment or dictating it through a good friend, straining to find words for something that takes some explaining. How many attempts did he make to start his Gospel? Was there a large pile of torn parchment all around his desk? Did he sweat to get these phrases out, or did they come freely and flow from his spirit? When did they start to build up in him? Was it when he first met Jesus, when he first heard his words and realized that he was listening to the Word?

In today's brief passage, John declares a truth that has gripped him: Jesus has made God known. If you have been following these readings through Advent and Christmas, you will be reading today's text on 6 January, the twelfth day of Christmas, also known as the feast of the Epiphany. The word 'epiphany' is a Greek word that means 'appearance' or 'shining forth'. It carries an implication that it involves something that has hitherto been hidden, and is now on show for all to see. And this is what John is communicating in his prologue, culminating in today's verses: God, through Jesus, is no longer hidden—he has been seen. He's made an appearance, and this appearance has filled the world with wonder and hope. To explain this epiphany a bit more, John talks about the contrast between law and grace. For the Jewish reader the law was vital. Moses had received the law at Sinai; its essence was in the words of the Ten Commandments, but it was filled out with many other requirements for every area of life, some recorded in the Torah (the first five books of the Bible) and some developed by the rabbis over the course of time. The law gave the people of God a great sense of security: you knew where you stood; you knew what was right and what was wrong; you knew what behaviour pleased God and what offended him; it gave order to society, and it gave you your bearings in life. However, the problem with the law is that it could make you feel that God was more like a High Court judge than a caring parent. If you went only by the law, then you could feel that God was looking down on you, scrutinizing every move you made and every thought that passed through your mind with a judgment as to whether it was right or wrong, holy or sinful. Life therefore was very much about appeasing God in the hope that when you died and approached the throne of heaven, God would find that your good works outweighed your bad in the scales of divine justice. The law bred a mentality that you got what you deserved.

This sense of a God of law is still very much around today. When someone goes through a hard time, and a friend looks accusingly at the skies and says 'What did she do to deserve that?', the question betrays a sense that God is a God who punishes people who behave badly and rewards those who behave well. That kind of thinking is law thinking. John says that there is another fundamental dimension to all of this, summed up in the word 'grace'.

John writes that grace and truth came through Jesus, this human who was born into the world as the epiphany of God. God manifested himself in a way that grace and truth were liberally released into the world. Truth is a strong theme of John's Gospel.

Jesus frequently preaches about it: true worshippers worship in spirit and *truth* (4:23); the *truth* will make you free (8:32); the devil preaches lies and there is no *truth* in him (8:44); Jesus is the way, the *truth* and the life (14:6); the Holy Spirit is the Spirit of *truth* (14:17; 15:26; 16:13); Jesus prays that his disciples will be made holy in the *truth* (17:17); he has a discussion with Pilate about the *truth* before his trial, with Pilate asking the fundamental philosophical question, 'but what is *truth*?' (18:38). We live in a world where it is often difficult to know what is true, what is false, whom to believe or not to believe. The wonderful thing about the coming of Jesus into this world, declares John, is that at last we have a measure for truth, and that is a great security.

But it is not truth on its own—it is truth and *grace*. In fact, not just grace, but 'grace upon grace' (1:16). It is grace so abundant that it will astonish you, a grace mountain or grace lake. What is grace? As a child I was taught it was 'God's Riches At Christ's Expense', and I still think that that's not a bad explanation. Grace is what happens when we love. It is the parent who watches a child misbehave and reprimands him but also sees into the child's heart, his vulnerability, his fears and his longings, and rushes to give him a consoling hug; it is that extraordinary ability some people have to forgive those who have caused much hurt; it is that determination to see love having the final say and the freedom to be generous rather than to demand rights. And when Christ came into the world, this ocean of grace was released. There are only three verses in this Gospel where the word *grace* appears, and they all come together in chapter 1, verses 14 to 17. Maybe John only mentions it these few times at the beginning of his Gospel because the rest of his book is entirely this message: God is on our side, and he came in the person of Jesus to prove it.

So John's prologue finishes with this wonderful theme of epiphany—Jesus, who is close to the Father's heart, has made God known to us (1:18). It is the overture to his Gospel, carrying this fundamental theme that God has come to humankind, revealing to us what is really true, and bringing that ocean of grace, which offers healing to every broken place of his beloved world. If you read on in John's Gospel you will see these themes lived out in the stories of Jesus and ultimately in his death and in his wonderful conquering of death. You meet ordinary men and women who encounter Jesus and are in turn brought near to the Father's heart: they are drawn by him, captivated by him, puzzled by him, annoyed by him, and always loved unconditionally by him. They met a Galilean who ate roast lamb at festivals and drank wine at weddings, who hugged lepers in the streets and taught thousands in the hills, who laughed at human jokes and wept at human gravesides.

John, as did Matthew, Luke and Mark, wrote his Gospel because he firmly believed that these were stories that did not just have relevance to a few first-century people who happened to live in first-century Palestine. They knew they had met someone who was much more than a wise teacher and wonder worker. The deeper instincts in them had told them that they had seen, smelt, felt and heard none other than God Almighty in the bones and flesh of this carpenter's son, and they gave their lives to writing and preaching about him so that the likes of you and me could have our own epiphanies— moments of revelation, moments when the Jesus written on the pages of an old book becomes more real than any reality, more true than any truth, and more full of love and grace than any love or grace that we have encountered.

At the beginning of this book I quoted Sister Stan who wrote, 'Hope is daring, courageous; it has the audacity to reach a hand into the darkness and come out with a handful of light.' In these last weeks we have explored some Bible passages and met some of the extraordinary characters in those stories, and I feel we have caught sight of the courage that is willing to reach into the darkness to find the handful of light. I think John, with his great love for the light, would encourage us always to take the risk and go on searching for this hope, even if we collect a few bruises as we fumble in the dark. And he would want us to do so in the knowledge that the cup of God's grace is always fuller than we think, and the light that we grasp with our weary hands in those shadowy places is a light that no darkness can ever extinguish.

Reflection

As you look back over the past 37 readings, which one stands out for you the most? What makes it so significant for you? What are your thoughts about hope now, as you come to the end of this book?

Prayer

Lord, when I encounter the dark places of this world, give me the courage to reach out my hand and don't let me withdraw it until I have caught hold of the light.

Notes

1 Stanislaus Kennedy, *Gardening the Soul*, Simon & Schuster, 2001, reading for 21 March.
2 For more information see www.soulcafe.co.uk.
3 Walter Brueggemann, *Hopeful Imagination*, Fortress Press, 1986, p. 9.
4 C.S. Lewis, *A Grief Observed*, Faber, 1961, p. 43.
5 Also published in Sue Watterson (ed.), *Looking Through Glass*, Veritas Publ., 2006, p. 37.
6 Frederick Buechner, *Telling the Truth*, Harper Collins, 1977, p. 43.
7 William Shakespeare, *King Lear*, Act V, scene III.
8 Michael Mayne, *An Enduring Melody*, DLT, 2006, p. 42.
9 Charles Wesley (1707–88), 'Come, Thou Long-Expected Jesus'.
10 For example, see Revelation 21:1.
11 From the poem 'Waste' in *The Unutterable Beauty* by G.A. Studdert Kennedy, Mowbray, 1983, p. 29.
12 Michael Grundy, *'Woodbine Willie' Fiery Glow in the Darkness*, Worcester City Council, p. 18.
13 From *The Unutterable Beauty* by Studdert Kennedy, p. 89.
14 See my book *Wild Beasts and Angels: Remaining human in the healing ministry*, DLT, 2000.
15 Ben Okri, 'An African Elegy', 1990, in *A African Elegy*, Vintage, 1997.
16 *The Shawshank Redemption*, director: Frank Darabont, 1994.
17 *The Return of the King*, director: Peter Jackson, 2003, based on *The Lord of the Rings* by J.R.R. Tolkien.
18 John Cennick and Charles Wesley, from the hymn 'Lo! He comes with clouds descending'.
19 Quoted in Ken Gire, *The Weathering Grace of God*, Servant Publications, 2001, p.106.
20 For the colour version of this picture go to www.awrc4ct.org/artwork/hanna/canvas/3554005.htm. For information about Hanna Varghese, see her website www.asianchristianart.org/profile/HVarghese/HVarghese.html.
21 Charles Wesley (1707–88), from the hymn 'Love divine, all loves excelling'.
22 Graham Kendrick, 'Thorns in the Straw', © 1994 Make Way Music, www.grahamkendrick.co.uk.
23 John Marriott (1780–1825), from the hymn 'Thou whose almighty word'.
24 See Suetonius, *Life of Vespasian 4.5* and Tacitus, *Histories 5.13*.
25 Vincent J. Donovan, *Christianity Rediscovered, SCM*, third edition, 2006. Preface to second edition, p. XIX.
26 Because Jesus was born in the time of Herod the Great, we know that Jesus must have been born by 4BC. Herod's murder of the children under two years old (Matthew 2:16) suggests Jesus was no older than two at that time.
27 Daniel Goleman, *Emotional Intelligence,* Bantam, 1995.
28 'There will be a Light', from the album *There will be a Light* by Ben Harper and The Blind Boys of Alabama, EMI, 2004.
29 C.S. Lewis, *The Voyage of the Dawn Treader,* Puffin, 1965, pp. 194–195.
30 Charles Wesley (1707–88), from the hymn 'Christ, whose glory fills the skies'.
31 Buechner, *Telling the Truth,* p. 94.
32 Buechner, *Telling the Truth,* pp. 96–97.
33 Yunna Morits, 'Bad Weather in Dickson Bay' in *Post-War Russian Poetry,* Penguin, 1974, p. 246.
34 Mary Craig, *Candles in the Dark,* Spire, 1984, p. 136.